BEYOND THE TIGER MOM

CONTENTS

Homecoming

In early 2010, my husband, children, and I packed up all our stuff, waved goodbye to our cramped apartment in Manhattan, and flew across the world to Singapore. This wasn't my first cross-continental move: I was born and raised in India, but as a teenager, I moved to the US for college, and then stayed on there for graduate school and work. After fifteen years in the US, I found myself hungering for "home." I was yearning for tropical sun and heat, for the sounds of Tamil and Hindi, for *idli-dosa* breakfasts, and for the color and chaos of India.

Since home—India—wasn't really an option for my husband in terms of his career, we settled on Singapore, a tropical island and a global city that's just a short flight from India. Sight unseen, my husband and I, along with our two young children, arrived in Singapore right before Chinese New Year. Amidst deafening drumbeats and colorful red and yellow lion dances, we ushered in the Year of the Tiger and began a new phase in our lives.

As an Indian in Singapore, I felt at home. It was as comfortable as a soft couch, and like the smell of jasmine flowers and *garam masala*, everything on the island felt familiar. Besides having the tropical heat and color in common, Singaporean and Indian cultures, too, are very much alike. Family and filial piety are of supreme importance; kids are expected to obey and respect their elders; every older person is an "auntie" or an "uncle"; and exams dominate the lives of young children and their families.

Six months after I arrived in Singapore, I began teaching high-school English at an elite international school on the island. My students came from a wide range of backgrounds: a third of them were East Asian, another third were South Asian (mostly Indian), and the rest were Western (European, Australian, and American). At my first set of student-teacher conferences, I was taken aback when an Indian mother turned to me and said, "Please be stricter with my son. He needs a firm hand, and he needs to take his studies much more seriously." I had thought her son was doing just fine, but she clearly thought he could do much better. Later, at another parent conference that same evening, a Chinese mother whose English was not very good bowed low and said politely, "You must be thirsty from talking to so many parents." I nodded, and she immediately ordered her ninth-grade son, who was attending the conference so that he could translate if necessary, to run and get me some water. She proceeded to thank me profusely for teaching her son. I was struck by how different these conversations were from the parent conferences that I had experienced in the US. As I began to spend more time interacting with East Asian and South Asian students and parents, and increasingly with local Singaporean families, I found myself reflecting on the way that these families viewed childhood, parenting, education, and the very purpose of life itself. I became increasingly interested in the Asian reverence for education, the nature of parent-child relationships, the number of hours that children spent on academic work, and the importance given to both mathematics and memorization. What values did these Asian families—both Asian expats and local Singaporeans—hold; where did they originate; and how did they shape and dictate the decisions that parents and students made? Is there anything that Western parents struggling to discipline or motivate their children can learn from Eastern parenting and education? And if so, what is it? These are some of the questions that this book seeks to address.

As a parent, I began to question my own paradigms of parenting and child development. When we moved to Singapore, my son was nearly five and my daughter was eighteen months old. We've been living in this little island nation for five years now; my son is almost ten, and my daughter is six. Both my kids think of Singapore as home and feel a deep attachment to the island. When we first arrived, I enrolled my son in the private international school where I teach, and placed my daughter in a local bilingual (Chinese-English) preschool. Once my daughter turned four, she, too, joined the international school where I teach. Though the curriculum and faculty at this school are distinctly Western, the student body is largely Asian, creating a multiplicity of cultural influences (as well as some cultural confusion) in my children's lives. Growing up in Singapore, attending an international school that offers them both Western and Eastern influences, and engaging with East Asian and South Asian friends and family on a daily basis, my children are exposed to both the East and the West. As a parent, I have found myself carefully considering the strengths and weaknesses of East and West, Asia and America, and I find myself often caught in the middle, wondering what script to adopt, what decision to make, and what kind of a parent I want to be. Throughout this book, I trace my own journey as a parent and an educator, raising questions and reflecting upon the ways in which the cultures I have inhabited have shaped my parenting attitudes and decisions. **This book's thesis is that Western and Eastern parenting philosophies have vastly different strengths and weaknesses; therefore, parents on either side of the world can learn from each other—and in order to truly raise successful children in a global world, perhaps they *need* to learn from each other and blend the best of both worlds together.** This book offers research-backed suggestions on how to combine the best aspects of Asian and American parenting and education philosophies. I hope you will find my ideas practical, useful, and inspiring, no matter where you are in the world.

HOMECOMING

I was born in the South Indian city of Chennai to an American mother and a South Indian father. Though I spent a few years of my early childhood in the US, I was a Chennai girl, born and raised, and even today, I feel most whole and complete when I am in Chennai. I attended Sishya, an Indian school, where I completed my ICSE (Indian Certificate of Secondary Education) exams at the end of tenth grade. I have vivid memories of standing up when the teacher entered the room and chanting, "Good morning, Ma'am," in unison with my classmates. She would reply, "Good morning, children," and then tell us to be seated. After this formal greeting, we would begin our lesson. Respect for teachers was explicitly built into every class. We had to stand up to address a teacher, and we always called our teachers "ma'am" and "sir." When I think back to my school days, I remember tests and exams, sports days and parades, school plays and elocution contests, rain holidays in the monsoon, and long hours of tuition in Hindi and math. Most importantly, I remember strong friendships with my peers and good relationships with my teachers.

After my tenth-grade exams, I attended a beautiful international boarding school in the Nilgiri hills of India. Surrounded by mist and mountains, Kodaikanal International was started by American missionaries as an American school, but over the years it morphed into an international school that attracted students from India, Bangladesh, Sri Lanka, and the Middle East. We also had Koreans, Swedes, and Americans. Although the student body was largely South Asian, the faculty was very international, and the culture of the school was far more Western than that of Sishya. No more "ma'am" and "sir"; we called teachers by their last names. No more standing up when teachers entered the room. At Kodai, we slouched and lounged in our chairs when we spoke with teachers.

While I loved India as a child and love it still, like many Indian teens, I was enamored of all the West had to offer. As a teenager in India in the early 1990s, I assumed that everything American was ultra-cool: from cheeseburgers at McDonald's to TV sitcoms like *Who's the Boss* and *The Cosby Show,* all things quintessentially American fascinated me. Additionally, my mother, an American of German and Dutch descent, wanted me to study in America and understand the country of her birth and childhood. So, as a teenager, I left India and travelled to the US, and then spent fifteen years there studying and teaching.

My teaching experiences in the US spanned a range far wider than that of most American teachers. I began my teaching career with Teach for America, an organization that places qualified college graduates in some of the nation's most underserved and challenging schools for two years. I taught at Northeast Middle School in Baltimore, a very tough middle school that served mostly African-American students from low-income neighborhoods. I am not sure whether my students learned anything from me, but I certainly underwent a steep learning curve over the course of those two difficult years. I learned a tremendous amount about the politics of race and class in America. I read huge amounts of African-American literature and history in an effort to understand the origins of the issues that my students confronted. It took me a while to understand my students and connect with them. My students, in turn, didn't really know what to make of me.

One kid asked me, "Ms. T, what are you?"

I was confused. "What do you mean?" I responded.

"I mean, are you black, white, or Puerto Rican? We can't figure you out."

While they were trying to figure me out, I was trying to find my bearings in a world and a language that were entirely new to me. Initially, the way my students spoke English sounded awful to me. By the end of two years, however, I found myself feeling tremendous affection toward the way they spoke. The experience convinced me that what one thinks sounds right or wrong is entirely a function of conditioning, and that standard English is no better or worse than other variants of English. Over the course of two years, I forged relationships with both students and colleagues, and in the process, I gained a unique glimpse into another side of America.

After my baptism by fire in Baltimore, I attended Harvard University for graduate school, and then went on to teach in some of America's best private schools. I learned about white America, power and privilege, and progressive pedagogies. I learned how to facilitate provocative discussions and design college-level English courses for highly competitive high school students. **American schools, at their best, are outstanding.** While public education in America is plagued by many issues, America's top private schools, like the Winsor School in Boston, where I taught for three years, are unbeatable in the quality of education they offer students. The faculty at Winsor were deeply intellectual and wholly committed to teaching, and the students were motivated and thoughtful. The program offered students both academic rigor and creativity.

I gave birth to both my children in the US. Determined to be the best mother I could, I turned to American books on parenting for advice. I read these books fairly unquestioningly; they were, after all, written by "experts" on early childhood, and seemed very authoritative. I read about the importance of free play and the need to cultivate independence. I was determined not to "stress" my children and "kill their love of learning" by making them do any sort of uncreative "drill" work. Instead of disciplining my children by saying "no," I tried to use as much "positive reinforcement" as I possibly could and offered my children as many "choices" as I possibly could. The American experts offered me scripts that involved asking my children what they wanted and then catering to *their* desires and choices as much as I possibly could. As a result, when I did say "no" to my children or lose my temper with them, I felt extreme guilt. (Was I damaging them terribly? Was I hindering their creativity and freedom of expression and sense of agency?) In book after book, I read about the power of language-rich environments, and I began not only reading to my children every day but also talking to my children *all* the time, using as rich a vocabulary as I possibly could. American parenting, I found, was absolutely and utterly exhausting. And, as I focused on "empowering" my own children, I found that, as a parent, I was becoming increasingly disempowered. My young son clearly had his "sense of agency," but my own sense of agency seemed totally subsumed by his. At the time, though, immersed in American parenting and education rhetoric as I was, it seemed totally normal for me to relinquish my own parental power in order to empower my three-year old son.

Simultaneously, I felt tremendous pressure to make my son "independent" very quickly. Whereas children in Asia often sleep with their parents or grandparents for many years, my American doctor and my American friends all advised me to put my infant son in a crib in a separate room so that he could begin learning to be independent. Similarly, children in Asia are fed, dressed, and helped by parents and elders throughout their childhoods, but children in the US are expected to do everything on their own from very early on. Since leaving the US, I have spent a lot of time thinking about the various pressures and messages that American parents experience, and the long-term effects of these messages. The desire to make children "independent" seems to me a particularly Western obsession; most of the Asian parents I've encountered—both South Asians and East Asians—seem unconcerned with independence. If anything, they seem to value interdependence and attachment far more than independence.

Over the years I spent in the US, the way I saw the world became increasingly America-centric. America shaped my beliefs about education and parenting, and I assumed that American research about children and childhood was universal. With very little questioning or skepticism, I wholeheartedly endorsed American paradigms, and as a result, when I thought about schools and families back home in India, I felt a condescending disdain: they hadn't been educated as I had.

After fifteen years in the US, I had become an American parent and teacher. But I also found myself feeling increasingly confused and conflicted about my identity. Living and teaching in the US, I often felt as though I had become so distanced from my childhood self, my Indian self, that I had turned into another person altogether. I had acquired a strong American accent, which sometimes sounded terribly foreign and inauthentic to me. I had begun to think of the world as having America at its very center. India, the country that had loomed so large in my childhood, was relegated to the distant periphery of my new world. (Who in America really cares about India?) America and its politics assumed tremendous significance in my life. I began to think of myself as a "person of color," and "an Asian/Indian-American." And simultaneously, I started feeling a deep need to recover my original, authentic identity–I wanted to go home. Or at the very least, I wanted to move closer to home. And so it was that my husband and I decided to move to Singapore.

It was a homecoming. Around me, magenta bougainvillea flowers shone bright in the tropical heat. I was surrounded by the natural landscape of my childhood, the birdcalls that used to wake me up as a child, the flowers that I took for granted when I grew up. Over the years, I have become keenly aware of how the natural landscapes of our childhoods become deeply ingrained in our psyches. Often, during my fifteen years in the US, particularly in the middle of harsh, cold winters, my body would ache for sun and heat and color.

Back in hot and tropical Asia, a mere four-hour flight away from my childhood home of Chennai, surrounded by frangipani flowers and *koel* birds, I began to peel off the Americanized layers of my identity and rediscover my Indian-Asian self. In the process, I also learned a tremendous amount about my newly adopted home, Singapore.

MOVING TO SINGAPORE

Singapore is a fascinating country. A tiny island, it is like America in the sense that it, too, is a nation of immigrants. Singapore was originally part of Malaysia, and the indigenous population is Malay. Over the last two centuries, however, a large number of Chinese and Indian immigrants moved to Singapore, making it an Asian melting pot, an island that blended influences from both East Asia and South Asia. Singapore was forced to break away from Malaysia and become an independent nation in 1965. It now has a majority Chinese population with smaller Indian and Malay minorities, as well as a growing expatriate population from around the world. It is a very diverse and cosmopolitan city, and children across the island, whether they attend local schools, Indian schools, or International schools, benefit from a global environment. Best known for its rapid economic development, Singapore went from being a small developing nation whose population lived in *kampongs* (communal villages) to being a highly developed nation with a very well-educated and urbanized population in just three decades. Today, it is a clean, safe, and rich city that boasts a GNI (Gross National Income) of $52,986 USD.[1]

Singapore suffered from terrible race riots in the 1960s, and since then the government has made a tremendous effort to create a pan-Asian Singaporean identity. The government literally legislates racial harmony on the island by requiring people of different races to live together in government-subsidized housing complexes, and by requiring children of all races to attend schools together. By desegregating housing and schooling and by using the media to promote a unified population, the government has ensured that the race riots of the '60s won't reoccur.

Language, too, unifies people on the island. Everyone learns English and everyone speaks it in the same way: with a sing-song intonation and with added *"lahs"* for emphasis. The local version of English is supremely efficient. Why say, "Can I go to Orchard Road?" when you could just say "Orchard Road, can *lah*?" This colorful variant of English, which borrows from Chinese (Mandarin, Hokkien, and other dialects) as well as Malay and Tamil, is called Singlish.

---

1   Singapore Department of Statistics, *Singapore in Figures* (2015): 2–3.

SOURCES OF INFORMATION

While I spoke with a wide range of parents and students from different Asian countries for this book, **my sample size was not large enough for me to make any definitive statements about Asians in general or even Asians in Singapore; in fact, no sample size would justify these kinds of generalizations.** While Singapore is a lovely Asian melting pot with parents who trace their roots to China, India, and the Malay Peninsula, it is not in any way representative of all of Asia. I know that, just as Western views on childhood, parenting, education, and family span a wide range, so too do Asian views. I'm also well aware of the fact that there are many differences between Asian countries as there are between Western nations. Speaking about "Asia" as if it were one monolithic entity is clearly problematic, as is speaking about the "West." Japanese educational systems, values, and parenting styles are significantly different from Chinese ones, for example; just as American educational systems, values, and parenting styles are significantly different from French, British, and German ones. Within Singapore, too, parenting styles and beliefs differ widely. To avoid the problems inherent in making any kind of blanket statement, I have tried hard to tell individual stories instead of making broad generalizations. On occasion, however, I do generalize, because there are some characteristic patterns in different parts of the world—albeit with many, many exceptions in every case.

Furthermore, the students and parents I interact with all live in Singapore and speak English fluently. Most of them tend to be well-educated and affluent "global Asians," or Asians who have had exposure to various parts of the world. Clearly, they represent only a minuscule sliver of Asia. Many of the conversations that I quote in this book would be irrelevant and meaningless to the millions of Asians who are struggling to make ends meet and provide their children with basic access to education and health care. **I am well aware that this book is not in any way representative of Asia on the whole, or even of all Asian parents in Singapore: no book ever could be.**

This book is a journey into the personal stories of a range of English-speaking Chinese, Indian, and Malay mothers living in Singapore today. Through these highly individualized accounts, it seeks to create some understanding of the issues faced by middle- and upper-middle-class parents and educators on the island and across Asia. Additionally, the book examines my own journey as an educator and parent who has an Asian (Indian) background but has worked primarily in Western schools. It examines the dilemmas I have faced both in the classroom and at home in trying to reconcile the different perspectives from East and West and seek that perfect blend or balance of both Eastern and Western strengths.

Additionally, I have had the privilege of interviewing high-performing students in their final year of high school at some of Singapore's top junior colleges, including Hwa Chong Institution, the Anglo-Chinese School, Raffles Girls' School, and Dunman High School. My extensive conversations with these impressive young people gave me wonderful insights into their educational experiences, their aspirations, their home lives, and their values. I have also, through my own personal network, had numerous informal conversations with a range of young people in other local schools.

In addition to my personal and professional conversations with students and parents, I conducted formal interviews with forty mothers (Chinese and Indian) and a handful of my own Asian students. In my formal interviews, I tried to talk to a range of mothers with children in local Singapore schools and international schools. I also met informally with schoolteachers and school leaders who work in Singapore schools to discuss their thoughts on education. Finally, I formally interviewed Mrs. Clarinda Choh, head of gifted education at Hwa Chong Institution; Mr. Shane Kwek, a senior administrator at Innova Junior College; Dr. Kirpal Singh, professor at Singapore Management University; Dr. Gavin Jones, professor at the National University of Singapore; and Dr. Jason Tan, professor at the National Institute of Education in Singapore to further my understanding of education policy and social/family trends in Singapore and in Asia as a whole.

In addition to my interviews and conversations in Singapore, I have drawn on my own experiences growing up in India and attending Indian schools. I have also drawn on the interactions and conversations I've had with my friends in Chennai and their children. The views I put forth in this book are based entirely on my own experiences, observations, interviews, and conversations.

I have changed the names of all the parents and students whom I quote and cite in order to protect their privacy.

PART 1

ACADEMICS

Raising Strong Mathematicians, Passionate Readers, and Knowledgeable Thinkers

Such pure ghee in the milk!
Without churning,
How will the butter emerge?

Such fire in the heart of the twig!
Without being struck,
How will it ignite?

—**Kabir** (c. 1440–1518)

CHAPTER 1

Why Are All the Asian Kids on the Math Team?

"AND WHAT DO YOU DO FOR MATH?"

A few months after my arrival in Singapore, an old high school friend came to visit. Shreya grew up in Mumbai, and we had met at boarding school in India. Smart, logical, and analytical, Shreya won prize after prize for her academic skills when we were in high school. She went on to attend college and graduate school in the US before embarking on a successful career in finance. When Shreya came to visit me, she was expecting her first child, and she was full of questions about parenting and education.

We ate lunch together at a teeming hawker center in Singapore. As our eyes watered from the heat and spice of *laksa* noodle soup, I told her, proudly, about all the activities I did with my children: I read to them, I immersed them in a language-rich environment, I took them to museum exhibits and concerts for children, and, of course, I played lots of imaginative games with them. I was sure that I was doing everything right because I was following all the sage parenting advice that fills Western books on children and education; every book I had ever looked at said that the single most important thing a parent can do for her child is to read aloud to him on a daily basis. And after fifteen years in America, I had become an American parent.

After I finished, Shreya looked at me quizzically and said, "That sounds great. *But what do you do for math?*"

At the time, I thought that Shreya's question, *"What do you do for math?"* was a mere reflection of her own mathematical inclinations. But I was wrong.

As I became more settled in Singapore, I began hanging out with lots of other Indian moms. After fifteen years of constantly trying to assimilate and be "American," I could now just be myself. I didn't have to try to fit in or feel like the odd mom out. We would meet in the playground while our kids ran around and climbed on the jungle gym, or sometimes we'd chat over chai in each others' living rooms. Like moms around the world, we often discussed our children. All of us were concerned about our kids' social, emotional, physical, and cognitive development. Often we'd discuss what kinds of activities we did with our kids, and invariably, during these conversations, I would find myself faced with the question, *"And what do you do for math?"* I realized that this was in no way unique to Shreya; it is, in fact, a question that many of the Indian mothers I met in Singapore think about a lot.

As my social network began to expand, I met many Chinese-Singaporean moms, and I found that many of these mothers, too, were fairly obsessed with this very same question: *And what do you do for math?* Mothers here seemed to believe that strong math foundations must be built in the first ten years of a child's life. At one birthday party, I found myself talking to two Chinese-Singaporean moms while our kids watched a magician take silk handkerchiefs out of his ears. Our entire conversation revolved around helping our (very young) children develop strong math foundations. What kinds of activities work? What kinds of curricula and math enrichment? Should kids attend after-school classes at centers like Kumon or Abacus, or should they focus on Singapore math workbooks at home?

Having just spent fifteen years immersed in American education systems, I was honestly surprised by the emphasis that so many of the Indian and Chinese mothers I met placed on math. In the

US, early childhood and elementary education focuses largely on language and social skills. As an avid reader of American books on education and parenting, I had found vast quantities of material on language development and the need to raise children in a "print-rich, language-rich environment," but little or no mention of early math skills. Similarly, in my many conversations with American mothers and colleagues, the question of math rarely came up, and not once in America was I ever asked what I did for math.

Around the same time that I was becoming increasingly familiar with the Asian-mom obsession with math, I happened to supervise some exams at the international school where I taught. At one point, I was overseeing the "Additional (Advanced) Math" exam, which was taken by mathematically precocious ninth graders. These kids were in the top 15 percent of their class for math, so they took the International General Certificate of Secondary Education (IGCSE) math exam at the end of the ninth grade instead of waiting until the end of the tenth grade. As I paced up and down the aisles of the spacious exam hall, I noticed that every face was Asian.

I knew all the stereotypes surrounding Asian kids and math. And truth be told, as an English teacher of Indian origin, I knew that I was an anomaly: in my experience, very few Indians who have other options choose to study and teach subjects in the humanities or arts. When I was growing up in Chennai, there was always an aura around math and science. That was what the smart kids did; the humanities were for the kids who couldn't cut it in math class. In Indian schools, students choose between three academic tracks when they finish their tenth-grade exams: Science, Business/Commerce, and Arts/Humanities. These tracks invariably determine the college options and career choices open to students down the road. When I completed my tenth-grade exams in India, most of my high-performing peers pursued the sciences for their eleventh and twelfth grades, and the rest studied economics or commerce. In fact, there was so little demand for subjects in the arts and humanities at Sishya, the school I attended in Chennai, that the school didn't even offer an Arts/Humanities track for eleventh and twelfth graders. (The school now has a Humanities track, though it still attracts fewer students than the Science and Business/Commerce tracks do.) At the time, I didn't question the natural progression of bright students into the Science track. After tenth grade, I left Sishya and attended an international boarding school where I completed the International Baccalaureate (IB) diploma. Despite being drawn to the humanities, I chose to study chemistry and biology at the IB level because I had been conditioned to think—perhaps subconsciously—that high-performing students should study the sciences. It was only when I got to college in the US that I began to pursue an English major and take classes in the humanities.

The Asian reverence for math and science was reinforced during my college years. While in college in the US, I spent a lot of time with other international students, many of them from Asia. With very few exceptions, my Asian peers chose to major in either STEM (Science, Technology, Engineering, and Math) fields or economics. Yet I hadn't really thought about the roots of these trends until I landed in Singapore and began interacting with Indian and Chinese mothers who cared so deeply about their children's math education.

As I began to talk to parents and educators, I gained many insights into the strong STEM preference that exists among students and families in Singapore. In an interesting conversation with Clarinda Choh, head of the gifted education program at Hwa Chong Institution in Singapore, I learned that the top students there overwhelmingly choose STEM subjects and tracks over others. Similarly, as I investigated Singapore's local school curriculum in more detail, I noticed that at the primary level, the core (tested) subjects include English, math, "mother tongue," and science, but not the humanities and arts.

Fascinated by the mathematical bent of the parents and students I encountered in Singapore, I began to research numerous statistics about Asians and math: which kids make the final cut in the prestigious Intel science competitions that reward kids for their original scientific inventions? Who are the people getting PhDs in STEM fields in America? In international schools and American schools, which kids are participating in math and science competitions? Which countries are topping the charts in math and science tests?

Here are some of my findings. In the 2013 Intel Science Talent Search held in America, exactly 50 percent of the 40 finalists had either an East Asian or South Asian last name. Three of the top ten winners were Asian. In the 2014 Intel Search, 57 percent of the finalists had either an East Asian or South Asian name. These numbers were similar in previous years as well. In the last decade, roughly half of the finalists and semifinalists in this competition have been Asian-American kids. Given that in 2013, according to the US Census Bureau, only 5.1 percent of Americans identified themselves as completely Asian, the high Asian success rates in the Intel Science Talent Search are surprising.

In other competitions in the US, from Mathcounts to the Physics Olympiads to the Siemens Math and Science Competition, Asians dominate as well. Mathcounts, an American math contest for middle-school students, has Asian-American kids of East or South Asian descent winning the top spot every year. In 2013, the winner was Alec Sun; the runner-up was Ashwin Sah. The two semifinalists were Guanpeg Xu and Franklyn Wang. In 2014, the winner was Swapnil Garg, and the runners-up were Kevin Liu and Daniel Zhu.

American engineering schools tend to attract a disproportionate number of Asian students from India and China, often alarming American educators and fuelling debates on why American students don't want to pursue STEM degrees like their foreign counterparts. In his provocative and politically incorrect book *Teaching Minds*, professor Roger Schank, founder of the Institute for the Learning Sciences at Northwestern University, describes America's fears of Asian dominance in math and STEM fields by saying, "As a person who was involved with graduate admissions for thirty years at three of the top ten universities in the country, I know what this hysteria is actually about. Nearly all applicants to graduate computer science programs (which is what I know—but it is true in most fields of engineering and science) are foreign nationals…China and India provide most of the applicants."[2]

Unsurprisingly, this phenomenon does not just apply within America; it's true on a global scale. As the PISA (Program for International Student Assessment, a test administered to fifteen-year-olds in sixty-five countries) tests routinely demonstrate, East Asian nations outperform the rest of the world on math tests by a significant margin. In the most recent PISA test (2012), Shanghai topped the charts for math with a score of 613, and Singapore came in second with 573. (In comparison, the US scored 481, and the UK scored 494). China routinely wins top place in the International Mathematical Olympiads. These successes extend beyond high school; Asians are now earning an increasing number of PhDs in STEM fields, and East Asian nations are pumping money and resources into scientific research.

In contrast to its East Asian neighbors, India performed abysmally in the 2009 PISA test, coming in at the very bottom of the international charts. The two states in India that participated in the test, Himachal Pradesh and Tamil Nadu, placed seventy-first and seventy-second out of seventy-three countries. As a result of this humiliatingly low performance, the Indian government withdrew India from the 2012 PISA tests. One can easily be misled by the mathematical success of Indian students outside of India, as well as the performance of Indian students from middle- and upper-class urban schools and universities (such as the renowned Indian Institute of Technology) within India. The impressive academic success of these elite Indians, Indian-Americans, and the larger Indian diaspora is not reflective of India's public (government-run) educational system, which is in a state of crisis. Plagued by debilitating poverty, poor nutrition and health care, and inadequate access to books, technology, and quality schools, the vast majority of Indian children are far behind their international peers when it comes to

---

2   Roger Schank, *Teaching Minds* (New York: Columbia University Press, 2011): 82.

math or any other academic subject. Given my own Indian roots, I find this situation tragic, and I wish that the Indian government would learn from its East Asian neighbors who have invested strategically in teacher education, curriculum development, and school infrastructure to ensure that *all* children have access to a quality education.

WHY DO ASIAN KIDS EXCEL AT MATH?

So everyone in both America and Asia seems aware of how well Asian students in Asia, as well as Asian-Americans, are doing in math. But *why* is this the case? The most popular explanation is the one posited by Malcolm Gladwell in his popular book *Outliers*: The Chinese do well in math because their number system is easier and more intuitive, and because they have developed a strong work ethic as a result of their history cultivating rice.

In his book *The Number Sense*, neuroscientist Stanislas Dehaene describes "the cost of speaking English." He explains how English number names are not only longer but also more difficult than their Chinese counterparts. Chinese number words can be uttered in less than one-quarter of a second, while the English equivalents take about one-third of a second. This enables Chinese speakers to hold far more digits in their memories at once. (No wonder they're great at mental math.) Furthermore, the number system in English is highly irregular. In contrast, East Asians have a logical counting system. Eleven is ten-one 十一. Twelve is ten-two 十二. Twenty-four is two-tens-four 二十四 and so on.[3]

The language theory sounds good, and it may give East Asians a small advantage over those who use more cumbersome number systems. Chinese, Korean, and Japanese speakers have the added advantage of developing better visual-spatial skills and concentration as they learn the thousands of complex characters one needs

---

3　Stanislas Dehaene, *The Number Sense: How the Mind Creates Mathematics* (New York: Oxford University Press, 2011): 89.

to know to be literate in these languages. However, this still doesn't explain why so many Asian-Americans or Singaporean kids (of Chinese, Indian, and Malay backgrounds) do so well at math: most of them speak English as a first language, and they think in English. So the difference in number systems shouldn't matter. And what about "global Indian kids"? Why are so many of these "global Indians" doing so well?

Many American educators and parents believe that Asian success in mathematics can be attributed to Asian school curricula. American "reform math" programs like Investigations and Everyday Math, they say, are not as systematic and mastery-oriented as Asian programs. These American programs encourage students to "discover" math for themselves and "construct their own understanding of mathematical concepts," and they often marginalize or ignore standard algorithms. Unlike Asian math programs, which combine hands-on activities with direct instruction and lots of drill and practice, contemporary American programs devalue practice and precision in favor of "discovery and exploration." Furthermore, critics of American math curricula point to the tremendous emphasis placed on language, as students are expected to *explain* steps and *discuss* different strategies to solve problems. In contrast, Singaporean students are expected to use number sentences, draw mathematical models, show their work, and solve the problems, but they are rarely asked to explain or discuss math problems in great detail. The assumption in Singapore is that if students can solve a range of problems correctly, they understand the concepts.

These American math methods, many of which are associated with the new Common Core standards in the US, have politicized math education considerably, bringing protests from many parents and even a number of well-known professors like Marina Ratner of Berkeley and James Milgram of Stanford, who claim that children need to learn standard procedures and concepts before they can begin to discover and create math on their own, and that all kids need to practice math enough to really master foundational concepts and internalize mathematical logic. Asian programs, they say, are more systematic, as they cover fewer topics but examine each one in greater depth and aim for mastery.

Furthermore, Asian programs tend to have more rigor and depth to them. A quick comparison of Singapore math texts with texts from the American Investigations and Everyday Math curricula reveals that the Singapore math problems tend to involve more steps and harder calculations, and they stick with one topic for far longer. In fact, some of the word problems (or problem sums, as they are widely known here) in Singapore math books are astoundingly difficult, as they require tremendous conceptual thought.

More rigorous math curricula at school, combined with a challenging exam system, could be part of the reason for Asian kids' success in math, but I still wasn't convinced. A lot of the Asian kids that I worked with had attended international schools that used Western curricula, and they still excelled at math. And what about all those Asian-American kids? They obviously attend American schools and follow American curricula, yet they tend to do well in math.The more I thought about it, the more I became convinced that the superior performance of many Asian kids in math and science has less to do with Chinese number systems or Asian school curricula and more to do with the families and cultures in which these kids grow up. They are raised by parents who spend a lot of time thinking about ways to build a strong mathematical foundation. They are raised in mathematical homes, where math is woven into the fabric of their lives from the time they begin talking. In other words, these kids spend a lot of time doing math.

WHAT ASIAN MOMS SAY ABOUT MATH

What do Asian mothers do for math? Well, let's start with some major qualifiers. Generalizing about Asian mothers, or even just Singaporean mothers, is utterly ludicrous. With a population of over 4 billion, Asia is astoundingly diverse in every way possible. Singapore, though it's a tiny island with a population of approximately 5.4 million, is still far too big and diverse to generalize about.

However, even with my limited sample of parents, definite patterns began to emerge, and I began to piece together some theories of my own about what "Asian math moms" do.

To begin with, the mothers I encountered genuinely believed that math is very important. This may sound insignificant, but it's not. In fact, I believe it may be the key to why so many Asian students excel at math: **they succeed because they value it.** Valuing math is not as obvious as it sounds. When I lived in the US, I didn't hear parents constantly talk about math. And even in Singapore, I rarely hear Western expats talking about math the way that Asians do. When a community values something deeply, it diverts resources and energy toward that thing. Of the mothers that I formally interviewed in Singapore, every single one said that they valued math, and that it was important to them that their children do well in it. In numerous informal conversations, too, mothers described the importance they attached to math. They also said that they communicate this value to their children very explicitly, so their kids also believe that math is extremely important.

Moreover, they believe strongly that when it comes to math, the first ten years of a child's life are critical. As Laura Tan, a Chinese-Singaporean mother, said, "I believe strongly in foundations. If kids have strong foundations, then later learning will be much easier." When I first started researching Asian parental attitudes toward math, I met with a group of Chinese teachers at the school where I work. One of them, who has a young child of her own, said earnestly, "We start our children on math very early, and we provide a lot of rigorous math instruction in the early years. With strong basics, everything else will fall into place." The other teachers nodded: foundations are critical.

One afternoon, I found myself sitting in an elegant living room, sipping tea and eating homemade *bhel puri* with four Indian mothers who had children ranging in age from four to fourteen. These ladies had agreed to speak with me about parenting and math, and one of them hosted the group in her house. The discussion was rich with insights, and occasionally with disagreements.

One mother spoke passionately about how frustrated she had been in high school in India because she found math baffling; she described feeling liberated when she began a college course in design and was finally able to drop math. Another mother insisted that one can never "drop math" because it is everywhere. She told a story about her brother, who found himself doing more math than he had bargained for even though he had a non-math job in the Indian army.

Another mother described how her daughter, who was not naturally talented in math, came home one day and announced that she had finally made it into the accelerated math group. Despite thinking that she should feel jubilant at the news, the mother actually felt bad, because she realized how much pressure her daughter had felt. The girl had really struggled to make it into this accelerated math group, and the emotional cost of this struggle seemed almost too high to the mother. "Why did I make her feel as though she *had* to get into that accelerated group?" she wondered aloud.

But one thing all the mothers agreed on was that math was important.

When I asked why, here are some of the reasons they gave:

- Math teaches kids to think logically and systematically.
- STEM fields hire more Asians and pay better than other fields. Math gives kids access to a whole host of lucrative job opportunities, from engineering and astrophysics to investment banking, molecular biology, and medicine. Math is the "critical filter" that decides who has access to higher-paying and more easily available jobs.
- Math is a universal language. Everyone is equal at the math table, because it is objective and value-neutral. In this sense, math is a fair game, open to all, regardless of a person's culture or background.
- Math rewards effort more than any other subject. All the mothers I spoke with reiterated the idea that success at math, especially at the school level, is a matter of dedication and practice. Mothers commented on the precision, logic, and objectivity of math,

saying that there is a "right answer" for each math problem; if a student studies and practices math enough, she will internalize mathematical logic, master the required procedures, and be able to solve the problem.

- Math is a "scoring subject": It's easy for kids to score high grades on a math test. On an English or humanities assignment, there is always something you can do better. On a math test, if you practice hard enough, you'll be able to solve the problems and get 100 percent.

Since these moms value math, they spend a lot of time on it. Pretty much every mom I spoke with did some amount of supplementary math with her elementary school children—either they send their kids to after-school enrichment classes like those run by Kumon or Abacus, or they sit down with their kids and work through math workbooks. Of the forty mothers I formally interviewed, a third do both.

MATH IN THE TWENTY-FIRST CENTURY: Asian anxiety and technological power

One of the first friends I made when I arrived in Singapore was Priya, a software engineer from Mumbai who had given up full-time work to raise her two sons. Priya and her husband, both engineers who see the world through scientific eyes, are raising their children in a highly mathematical and scientific home. When I asked Priya about her strong bias toward math and science (over the arts and humanities), she replied that both she and her husband believe that math and science are crucial for the twenty-first century. "Kids who understand math and science understand the highly scientific and technological world we live in...I want my kids to be able to understand the world they live in and navigate it successfully," she said.

I had to agree with her. As a non-math/science person myself, I often feel overwhelmed and intimidated by the world I live in. In the twenty-first century, many of us inhabit a highly advanced technological world full of machines that we don't really understand,

and our lives and lifestyles are entirely dependent on the scientists, engineers, and technicians who design, make, and fix our machines. The idea that we don't actually understand our world is both disturbing and disempowering. Priya is right. Even if your child has absolutely no intention of becoming an engineer or a scientist, math and science are the basis of the modern world, and feeling comfortable and empowered in this high-tech world demands a sound understanding of its mathematical and scientific foundation.

Perhaps even more than giving kids an understanding of the world they live in, math and science give people access to jobs. And for most Asian families, this matters intensely. The Indian and Chinese parents that I spoke with were acutely aware of the ferocious competition for jobs and money in both India and China. The numbers of young people in these countries are staggering. India is a remarkably young country; the current median age is twenty-five. And it's projected to become even younger; economists believe that over the next three decades, 50 percent of its population will

ASIAN PARENTS SPEAK OUT

"We want to push him as far as we possibly can"

"Aalok was born to be an engineer. When I took him to his first piano class, all the other kids were interested in the music. Our son, on the other hand, wanted to figure out how the piano worked. At the end of class, he peered into the piano, sat under it, and examined it from every angle. How did it work? That's an engineer in the making. You can tell a lot about a child by watching how he plays. Aalok can play with his Lego sets for hours. Literally hours. He forgets about food, sleep, everything, when he's engrossed in his Lego. He really loves building things and his buildings are becoming increasingly complex. We're doing everything we can to develop his talents. We're helping him prepare for the Singapore Math Olympiad, we do a lot of supplementary math with him, and we've already taught him quite a bit of simple programming. He has a high tolerance for mental work, so we just want to push him as far as we possibly can. I want him to see just how much he can do, how far his mind can go."   – **Tarun**, father of Aalok (nine) and Dilip (seven) be under the age of twenty-five. How is India going to create jobs for over half a billion young people? In contrast to India, China's population is aging fairly rapidly because of its one-child policy. In spite of this, with over a billion people, the Chinese, too, feel as though they are engaged in a desperate competition for jobs and money that very few people can actually win. In a *Time* magazine article, Gu Yong Qiang reported that in 2013 almost 7 million college graduates will be looking for jobs in China, the highest number ever recorded in the country's history. The report added that only 35 percent of soon-to-be college graduates in April, 2013, had found jobs, according to a survey by MyCOS, a data firm in Beijing. The situation for postgraduates was even more dire, with only 26 percent having signed an employment contract.[4]

Given that many Indians and Chinese are acutely anxious when it comes to the financial well-being of their progeny, it is unsurprising that they want to push their children into math and science, where the jobs and money are. In wealthier countries like Singapore, Japan, and Korea, parents are choosing to have fewer children than previous generations did, but the pressure to have "quality children" who can compete in a cutthroat world is intense. Strong math skills are often seen as one solid way to stay competitive.

As the economy becomes increasingly global, perhaps the narrow emphasis on math and STEM subjects in Asia will decelerate. In America, for example, a recent survey[5] revealed that an increasing number of second- and third-generation Asian-American students are choosing careers in the humanities and the arts. Similarly, Susan Chan, a Chinese-Singaporean mother, described the growing

---

4   Gu Yong Qiang, "In China, Higher Education Brings Few Guarantees," *Time* magazine (July 14, 2013).

5   Hao Li, "Asian Americans Increasingly Defy Stem Stereotypes," *International Business Times online* (August 6, 2010). http://www.ibtimes.com/asian-americans-increasingly-defying-stem-stereotype-246578). Ying Yi Ma, "Model Minority, Model for Whom? An investigation of Asian-American Students in Science/Engineering," *AAPI Nexus: Asian Americans & Pacific Islanders Policy, Practice and Community*, UCLA Asian American Studies Center (September 19, 2011).

popularity of the School of the Arts (SOTA) in Singapore. She said that when she was young, the arts were not viewed as a viable career option, but now, SOTA is an increasingly attractive option for students. The government is also trying to offer more nontraditional programs and career paths to students with non-academic interests. She expressed tremendous relief at this growing acceptance of the arts as a career choice, because her own daughter is artistically inclined but not very good at math.

As Susan Chan indicates, not every Asian child is interested in or strong at math, and not all Asian parents privilege math and STEM fields over the humanities and the arts. Both in India and in Singapore, I have encountered families (my own included) who are devoted to literature and the arts. As an English teacher, I sometimes hear my literary Asian students—South Asian and East Asian—joke about how they don't fit the cultural stereotypes. They feel moved and exhilarated by language and literature and, in contrast, somewhat frustrated by math.

The stereotype of educated Asian students being good at math, however, *is* backed by numbers: very high PISA math scores in East Asian nations, the high enrollment rates of East and South Asians in engineering colleges, and the disproportionate number of high-performing Asian students who study STEM subjects over the arts. Yet, like any stereotype, these numbers paint only part of the picture, offering only a limited view of a large and diverse community. Additionally, the stereotypes may also be self-fulfilling. Asian students may feel as though they *have* to be good at math and science, and are therefore driven into math and STEM and away from the arts and humanities. On a troubling note, these stereotypes may affect non-Asian students in damaging ways as well; they may assume, for example, that they won't be able to compete with Asian students in a math classroom, which could sabotage their chances of excelling at math. In his book *Whistling Vivaldi*,[6] Stanford professor

---

6   Claude Steele, *Whistling Vivaldi: How Stereotypes Affect Us and What We Can Do* (New York: W. W. Norton & Co., 2010): 90–94.

Claude Steele cites studies that show how the current slew of math stereotypes favoring Asian boys damages the performance of both non-Asian students and female students on math tests. Perhaps parents and educators need to make a particular effort to counter these stereotypes by reminding *all* students that success at math is a function of hard work and practice, not race or gender.

BUILDING MATHEMATICAL HOMES

The parents I interviewed here in Singapore—middle- and upper-class Asians—are an influential and successful group, and they offer all parents some vivid insights into what it takes to raise a child who excels in math. What do they do with their kids at home? How do they pass on their interest in math to their children?

As I talked to Priya in greater detail about what she did with her boys, I realized that she integrated math and science into the fabric of daily life in a number of ways. In other words, she built a math-rich home for them. Now, in the US, I had read over and over again about the importance of creating a print-and language-rich home for children, but here in Asia, I began to see many mothers working hard to create a **mathematically rich home** for their children. Mothers like Priya talked to their kids about numbers, shapes, and patterns from the get-go. They played math games when they were in the car or at the dinner table (guess the number, solve the mathematical riddle, add up the numbers on license plates as quickly as possible, calculate distance traveled, etc.). They taught their kids chess. They spent money and time on Lego sets, building blocks, tangrams, jigsaw puzzles, and board games. When they took the kids to the grocery store, they talked math: "If one apple costs 80 cents, how much will six apples cost?" When they rode the elevator, they talked math: "Look, we're riding up and down a number line. If we're on the fifth floor now, how many more floors till we get to the eleventh floor?"

I asked Lara, a Singaporean chartered accountant with a math-inclined son, how she had managed to raise a child who so clearly loved math. "What really matters is that I get him to notice the math that exists all around us," she replied. "When we go to the playground, for example, I ask him what he sees, and we talk about shapes and patterns. I'll point out an isosceles triangle to him, or we'll look at the shapes and patterns on the jungle gym. While kids need to know their numbers and be good at mental math, the fact is that when they are older they will all be using calculators to deal with numbers. So while workbooks and mental math practice are important, the more important thing is to make sure that they understand how to think logically, how to approach problems, how to see the math that is all around them. Math today is so much more than numbers. Kids need to see that they are surrounded by math."

Besides deliberately building a math-rich home, most of the Asian mothers I know also set to work making sure that their kids learned math early. Asian mothers—both South Asian and East Asian—*love* math workbooks. Unlike many Westerners who shun workbooks, claiming that too many drills will kill a child's love of learning, Asian moms, in my experience, adore them. They gain great satisfaction from watching their young children complete good old-fashioned drills. Looking at a sheet full of correctly solved math problems is tangible proof of learning that makes mothers feel reassured and happy. In addition to workbooks, many Asian mothers encourage their kids to do online math games and math drills.

When I first arrived in Singapore, local moms introduced me to stores that specialized in academic workbooks. Additionally, at certain special stores on the island, parents can purchase "past math exam papers" from some of Singapore's top schools. In fact, these "past math exams" have become so popular that parents can now order them by phone and have them delivered to their homes. In Singapore, at the primary (elementary) level, kids have to take a ninety-minute math exam at the end of each semester. These exams are not for the faint-hearted; they include a wide range of conceptually and procedurally rigorous problems. A lot of moms I know purchase packets of these practice exams for their kids, claiming that they not only help kids become mathematically proficient but also teach them how to focus and concentrate for extended periods of time. The act of sitting still and focusing on a demanding academic task for a long period of time is, according to many of the mothers and primary school teachers I talked with, the best way to help a child increase his or her ability to concentrate for a long time. Moreover, the time pressure of a test forces the child to stay focused—there is no room for daydreaming, distraction, or procrastination when the clock is ticking and the child has to solve forty-five problems. (In contrast, Western schools of education tell parents and teachers to cater to children's diminishing attention spans by making all learning activities "fun" and "short.") Almost every Indian and Chinese mom I know in Singapore spends some time sitting with their child and making sure that they do math workbook exercises.

The American fear of killing a child's love of learning by drilling her too much does not exist in Singapore, and I suspect this fear is unfounded. When I asked one Singaporean math educator if he uses the phrase "drill and kill," he responded, "No, we say that a certain amount of 'drill and *grill*' is necessary." As these kids get better and better at math, they don't hate or fear it. In fact, math immersion seems to have the opposite effect. Just as kids who read a lot develop a love of reading, it seems to me that many kids who do a lot of math develop a love of math. While Western education and parenting books and websites repeatedly warn parents of the dangers of "forcing" their children to do math, lest the child begins to resent and hate it, the Asian mothers I spoke with made comments such as, "If a child is weak at a subject, then he or she will naturally dislike it. If you want your child to enjoy a subject, you have to first help him or her become competent in it. We all like what we understand and are good at."

I've seen it over and over again at the school where I work. I come in to class, ready to start discussing poetry, and huddled around a desk is a group of math-oriented boys. (Unfortunately, these groups tend to be male; the gender inequity in higher-level math classes, though less acute in East Asia than in the West, is another story altogether.) They are arguing with each other in animated voices, making notes on a piece of paper as they talk. "What are you talking about?" I ask, interrupting their conversation in an effort to get my class started. "Sorry, Ms. T, we're talking about a math problem," they reply, showing me their books.

That's not math-phobia and math-hatred. That's math-love and math-pride.

I've seen the same phenomenon with my own children. When they work hard at a concept and master it, they begin to see it as fun. In contrast, when they are floundering and struggling with math concepts that they don't understand, they express dislike for the subject. The only way to reach the more satisfying mastery stage, however, is to first wade through that difficult and frustrating learning stage and then engage in substantial hours of practice. So shielding children from the frustration and challenge (and sometimes tedium) of learning and practicing new concepts won't make them hate math less; it will, conversely, make them hate math more. If it were drills that created math phobias, Asian kids would be intensely math-phobic, which they clearly aren't. Ironically, it's a lack of drilling, a lack of strong foundations, and a lack of mastery over basic mathematical concepts that creates and fuels math phobias.

IS EARLY MATH IMPORTANT? What the research says

While popular Western books on parenting and early childhood marginalize or ignore the importance of math, academic studies on early math reveal that it is just as important as early literacy. Just as early literacy primes kids for high achievement in school, so does early math. According to a recent study published in the Columbia University *Teachers' College Record*, researchers Amy Claessens of the University of Chicago and Mimi Engels of Vanderbilt University found that early mathematics knowledge and skills are the most important predictors not only of later math achievement in school, but also for achievement in other content areas (reading and science) and grade retention.[7] They go on to discuss research that shows how jigsaw puzzles and other spatial activities can improve mathematical thinking in early childhood.

Susan Levine, a psychologist at the University of Chicago, confirms the importance of early math skills. Her studies conclude that math skill at kindergarten entry is an even stronger predictor of later school achievement than reading skills or the ability to pay attention.[8] While there aren't anywhere near as many studies on the impact of early math skills as there are studies on early reading, the few that do exist all show a statistically significant correlation between early math achievement and later school success.

TEACHING VISUAL-SPATIAL SKILLS

If you want your child to have a strong mathematical foundation, you need to engage him in activities and games that will develop number sense, problem-solving skills, and visual-spatial skills. Research shows that all three strands are closely related to math success in school and beyond.

While most people already know that number sense and problem-solving abilities correlate directly with math achievement, they may not know that most students who excel in higher-level math and science also have good visual-spatial abilities; that is, the ability to understand shapes and manipulate objects in their minds. These skills are necessary to succeed in more abstract math and physics. Furthermore, there's a lot of research that suggests that visual-spatial skills can be improved significantly with deliberate practice. Since these skills are not explicitly taught in most schools, parents should pay particular attention to this area of math and science education early on, especially for their daughters.

---

7 Amy Claessens and Mimi Engel, "How Important Is Where You Start? Early Mathematics Knowledge and Later School Success," *Teachers College Record* Volume 115 (June 2013).

8 Susan Levine et al., "What Counts in the Development of Children's Number Knowledge?" *Developmental Psychology* 46, no. 5 (2011): 1309-.

In her book *Pink Brain, Blue Brain*, neuroscientist Lise Eliot explores the reasons for gender differences in spatial skills, where boys typically tend to outperform girls when tested. Eliot concludes that much of this difference is a function of the greater exposure to activities that build spatial skills that boys are given as compared to girls.[9] I see this bias all the time. My young son gets Lego sets as birthday presents from his friends. In contrast, my daughter gets crayons, play-jewelry, and craft kits from her friends, and none of them has ever suggested Legos as a play option. When I signed my son up for a Lego Robotics camp last summer, there was only one girl in the group of fifteen children. Clearly, boys get a lot more practice in this domain than girls do, and this could give boys a big advantage while negatively impacting girls' performance in math and science down the road. There's an easy solution to this: parents can buy Legos for their daughters, play blocks and tangrams with them, and sign them up for robotics classes.

SCRIPTING MATH EDUCATION: Are you wondering how to get your kids to do extra math?

After four years in Singapore, I have become much less of an American mother. Increasingly, I find myself drawing on my own childhood and my *desi* (Indian) roots as I parent my children. My interest in math has increased dramatically since I moved here. Where we used to spend all our time with words, my children and I now spend a fair bit of our time with numbers, shapes, and patterns, and I feel quite certain that regular math practice is good for kids. I encourage my kids to engage in fun math activities like Legos, puzzles, and games, but I also make them do some structured math worksheets every week. In fact—full disclosure here—I do supplementary math with my own children almost every weekend. We work through the Singapore math curriculum together,

---

9   Lise Eliot, *Pink Brain, Blue Brain: How Small Differences Grow into Troublesome Gaps—And What We Can Do About It* (New York: Houghton Mifflin Harcourt, 2009): 136, 137, 233–235.

which gives them lots of exposure to challenging, highly conceptual word problems.

When I first arrived in Singapore, conditioned as I was by American culture, I used to feel terribly guilty about "forcing" my children to do extra academic work, and I tried to gently cajole and bribe them into doing it. I tried everything I could to make math lessons fun and engaging, and I would stop when I felt they were getting tired or restless. Yet despite my gentle approach, often my attempts at getting my children to do extra math ended up with them crying and arguing with me. I would be left wondering how my Asian friends did it so easily; they made their elementary school kids do *hours* of math, seemingly without complaint. What was their secret? Doing extra math sounds perfectly easy, but how does a parent make a young child sit down for half an hour and work on word problems when she would rather be doing something else? I began informally discussing these issues with my Indian and Chinese friends, and their answers to my questions reminded me that the scripts and values that American culture gives its parents are not universal.

All of us parents are products of our cultures, and we live and breathe the parenting messages that permeate our cultures. These messages and scripts pervade our social interactions, the language of our schools, and the public messages in the media. They seep deep into our skin and bones in a way that makes them feel absolutely normal and right. It's very hard to see or question these cultural messages when we are steeped in them. Like the water that a fish swims in, the culture we live and parent in envelops and sustains us; it is virtually impossible for us to examine that culture objectively when we are swimming in it.

American parents and educators are told to give children choices, to respect their desires, to ask them questions as opposed to issuing orders, to refrain from pressuring or coercing them to do work they don't want to do, and to offer positive reinforcement all the time. Children are supposed to *want* to do the work—otherwise, they shouldn't have to do it. In contrast, the scripts that Asian culture offers its parents include statements, not questions, and orders, not requests. Children are routinely told what to do, and particularly when it comes to academic work, parents and educators don't spend much time asking them what they want or catering to those desires. Asian parents see these scripts as the natural order of the family and society; the elder has wisdom and a responsibility to teach and discipline the child, and the child needs to learn from those elders.

Interestingly, while American culture makes mothers feel guilty about pushing a child too hard academically and forcing him to do academic work that he may not want to do (for fear that he may then dislike the subject or suffer from lowered self-esteem), Asian culture makes mothers feel guilty about *not* pushing their children enough and abdicating what the larger culture sees as a mother's responsibility. In some of my interviews with mothers, I asked whether they ever felt guilty about making their children do extra academic work. My question was often received with absolute bewilderment. As one mother said, "But I feel I am doing my duty when I make my daughter study hard, because then I know that I am helping her learn and succeed. It's when I *don't* make my child do extra work that I feel terribly guilty."

Here are some of the statements that the parents I spoke with commonly make when they expect their children to do supplementary work. The most common refrain was, "I'm doing this for your own good. You will thank me when you're older." One Indian mother jokingly told me she says, "Math is supremely important. Do you know how important it is..." and then proceeds to lecture on about the importance of math in life until her children beg her to stop because they would rather just do the math than listen to her. Many of the mothers I spoke with use a common script that draws on the natural authority of the parent as well as the Asian value of filial piety. Mothers offered variations of the following script: **"I am your mother. Whatever I do, I do for your own good. I do everything in the world for you, and you need to be a good son/daughter and listen to me. You need to be a good son/daughter**

and respect your mother. No back-chat. Get to work." Or, "You are only a child. You don't understand how important your education is and what you need to do to be successful. I am much older, I know the importance of these skills." These messages are also reinforced by the broader Asian cultural milieu, which reinforces parental authority, filial piety, and a deep reverence for formal education.

Additionally, the Asian mothers I spoke with all reiterated the importance of "study routines" or "study schedules." If children assume that they will *have* to do supplementary math every Saturday morning, then they will accept it as part of their weekly routine. In many Asian families, the homework time carved into a child's schedule is seen as fairly sacred—parents make a big effort to ensure that children stick to these self-constructed study schedules. I recently met an American teacher who is married to a Chinese woman. I told him about the book I was writing and asked him what he and his wife do with their young daughter to help her with her academic work. He replied, "While my wife is not a stereotypical 'tiger mother,' she *is* somewhat fanatical about maintaining our daughter's study routines. She has times designated every day specifically for homework and studying, and if I try to engage my daughter in any alternative conversation or activity during these times, my wife goes a bit crazy. She thinks of this self-inflicted routine as sacred, while I'm much more spontaneous and relaxed." His description of his wife echoed much of what I'd heard from other Asian parents: those study routines are key to ensuring academic success in math and in other subjects.

Over the last five years, surrounded as I have been by Indian and Chinese culture, I have found myself reverting back to scripts from my own childhood in Chennai. While my own parents were very laissez-faire about parenting, the broader culture of India offered me strong scripts that included adults telling children what to do and children learning early on that they needed to respect their elders. Like old friends who reenter a person's life, these scripts seem familiar and comfortable; in many ways, they feel far more natural to me than the alternative scripts that I learned while I was in the US. I find myself increasingly using Asian scripts and study routines at home with my own children (albeit the gentler versions of them), and I find that these methods not only get my children to do supplementary academic work but also to ensure that they behave respectfully towards their elders. Despite occasional rebellions and protests, my children have now gotten used to doing their supplementary math work. Their math skills have improved, as have their concentration and focus. While my kids would still rather play, read, or watch television than do extra math, they are beginning to see the value in these sessions. Or so I hope.

When moms ask me what I do for math, I now have lots of good answers.

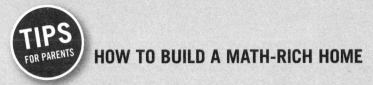

HOW TO BUILD A MATH-RICH HOME

For Number Sense:

- ■ **Play board games** such as Snakes 'n' Ladders, Yahtzee, and Monopoly.

- ■ **Invent and play games with dice**: Roll three dice and add the numbers, find the difference, etc.

- ■ **Play card games of all kinds**. My kids enjoyed simple games such as "Add the Cards," where each player picks out two cards from a pack and then has to add the numbers on their cards as quickly as they can. The player who can add the cards up the fastest wins the round and takes the cards. This can be modified in a range of ways (subtract the numbers, multiply, etc.) You can either take out the non-numerical cards or assign them an arbitrary numerical value.

- ■ **Use an abacus**. An abacus is a great tool for explaining place value and for introducing addition, subtraction, and mental math techniques. In Japan, many kids learn arithmetic and mental math on their *soroban* or abacus, becoming speedy human calculators. Abacus classes are popular across Asia today.

- ■ **Make up activities using a measuring tape**: measure your furniture; ask your kids to jump as far as they can (long jump), mark the starting line and the place where they land, and then get them to calculate how far they jumped (my son loved this game, and was constantly trying to break his own long jump record).

- ■ When you're in the car, play number games.

   1. *Guess the Number:* Think of a number, then give the kids some clues (it's a multiple of two, it's less than ten and more than four), then let them guess what number could it be.

   2. *Speed Addition:* give kids a list of numbers to add up, or ask them to add up all the numbers on license plates that you see, or ask them to arrange license-plate numbers in ascending or descending order.

   3. *How Far:* Have kids calculate the distance you've travelled.

- ■ Integrate math conversations into all your daily activities with children. Here are some ideas.

1. *Grocery-store math:* "Find me five tomatoes; now add two more tomatoes, how many do we have?" For older kids: "How much will 500g of ground meat will cost if 100g costs $2.20? How much will five bottles of shampoo cost if each bottle is $2.25?"

2. *Cooking Math:* "Can you add three eggs? Now, let's measure one cup of milk." For older kids, ask questions with fractions: "If we halve or double the quantities, how much will we need?"

3. *Elevator Math:* Get kids to add and subtract in the elevator, get them to recognize numbers, point out that you're riding up and down the number line.

▪ **Kumon workbooks and old-fashioned drills** in math workbooks will help kids master their math facts and understand basic algorithms for addition, subtraction, multiplication, and division.

▪ **Online programs like Hey Math, Splash Math, and IXL Math** can be good ways to get kids to practice math on a regular basis. A host of great online programs are available–from timed math drills to fun games and more conceptual problems. There are also some wonderful math apps available for iPads and iPhones. Dragon Box is a great app to teach children algebra (http://dragonbox-app.com/) Many mothers also recommend Khan Academy (www.khanacademy.org) for excellent math videos and assignments.

▪ **Get kids to decompose and recompose numbers** (mental math techniques); this will help them compute quickly and efficiently. For example, children can think of 47 + 83 as 40 + 80 + 7 + 3. By decomposing 47 into 40 and 7, mental calculations become easier.

▪ **You've got to make your kids practice, practice, practice** if you want to go the Asian way. The only way to really internalize number sense is to practice on a regular basis. In fact, research suggests that kids need to *over-practice* to make sure basic math facts like the multiplication tables are absolutely automatic, so that they can focus on the more conceptual parts of difficult problems later on.

For Problem Solving:

▪ **Have kids play games that require strategy**, such as Connect Four, Risk, and backgammon.

▪ **Play chess**–it's an excellent game for strategizing.

- **Give kids interesting word problems and math puzzles to solve**. Singapore math workbooks, which are now widely available in the US and are often used by homeschooling parents, are a great resource for this. Mathematics Olympiad books, which are available internationally, are wonderful too.)

- **Have kids write their own math problems**: In her book *What's Math Got To Do With It?* Stanford professor of math education Jo Boaler suggests giving students a "mathematical setting" such as an array of blocks or a bunch of rocks and stones, and then asking them to create their own math problems.[10]

- **Have kids solve math puzzles of any kind**: jigsaw puzzles, easy sudoku puzzles, etc.

- **Get kids to identify and extend patterns** (numbers, shapes, words, etc.). Give them an interesting numerical or shape-based pattern and then ask them to complete or extend the pattern. For example, 235, 242, 249...Can you extend the pattern? 15, 30, 90, 360...Can you extend the pattern?

- **Discuss possible problem-solving strategies that your children can use to solve problems**. In *What's Math Got To Do With It?* (pages 185–187), Boaler suggests talking to children about possible ways to solve complex problems: Draw the problem, make a chart with the numbers, try a smaller case, etc.

- **Give your children a wide range of problems to solve**. The key is variety. (Kumon, which is popular both in Asia and in the US, does not provide students with the variety and conceptual richness required to gain good problem-solving skills, though it does help students develop number sense and what I call "procedural math.")

- **Have kids play online math games**. There are many good ones, such as Math Blaster (www. knowledgeadventure.com) and Ice-cream Truck Math (www.sunburst.com), which kids might enjoy.

For Visual-Spatial Skills:

- **Give kids blocks, Legos, K'Nex**, and any other building activity that involves manipulating objects.

---

10 Jo Boaler, *What's Math Got To Do With It?* (Viking, 2008): 175–178.

■ **Give kids tangrams** (disembedding shapes and problem solving).

■ **Have kids try programming**: Scratch (scratch.mit.edu), Logo (logo. com/cat/browse/logo.html), Mindstorm: Lego-programming/robotics (mindstorms.lego.com), Tynker (tynker.com), and Microworlds (microworlds.com).

■ **Let kids play Tetris** (great online game for understanding how shapes fit together).

■ **Let kids play Minecraft** (warning: Kids may love this computer game, but some parents I interviewed claimed it was a gateway to a gaming addiction for their sons. Encourage it only in moderation).

■ **Have kids play building games like Blik Blok**.

■ **Work on origami with your kids**.

■ **Solve jigsaw puzzles with your kids**.

■ **Do measuring activities with your kids**.

■ **Do geometry activities** (drawing shapes, extending patterns, understanding shapes) with your kids.

■ **Encourage craft activities that involve shapes and building** (using recycled material to build a boat or a house, for example).

■ **Encourage kids to notice patterns in the world around you**: in nature, in architecture, in art.

■ **Encourage kids to try digital photography**.

CHAPTER 2

Raising Readers: Is West Really Best?

LET'S START WITH A-B-C

The sun was just setting, and the park was cool and pleasant. My son was kicking a ball around with some other kids, my daughter was making mud pies in the sandbox. And I, brand new to Singapore at the time, was chatting with three of the other moms who lived in my condo—part of my induction into the local mom-world.

"There's just no time...I have to find a way to get the kids to sleep earlier because they're just too tired in the morning, but somehow everything is so busy. I just don't know how to get them to bed earlier," said an Indian mom with two sons, aged four and six.

"What's their schedule like?" I asked, curious. "Well, they have classes right after school, and then they study for at least an hour, then at around six, they have some free time and on most days, I let them go out to play. By the time they finish playing with their friends, it's already seven. Then they have a bath and dinner and go straight to bed."

"But when do you read to them?" I asked.

"Read? Oh, they work on their reading during study time," she replied.

I looked around and asked the other two moms if they engaged in a bedtime story. They shook their heads. Reading, mostly of basic readers or school reading books, happened during study hour, they all agreed.

Almost a year later, I met my Singaporean friend Alisha, whose four-year-old son was enrolled in a local preschool. I had just put my two-year-old daughter into a local bilingual (Chinese-English) preschool as well, and I was eager to discuss the educational philosophies of these schools. As an English teacher, and as a parent who had been immersed in American parenting culture for so long, my first priority was reading. "How does your son's school engage kids in reading?" I asked.

"Well, the teacher reads them easy books, and asks the kids to come up and identify words in the book. For example, she'll say, "Can you come up and find the word *girl*? Remember, *guh- guh- guh.*"

"Does the teacher ever engage kids in a discussion of the story? Does she bring the story alive for the kids?" I asked. My friend looked at me a bit skeptically, "Not much, the focus is on phonics. She teaches kids how to read." I thought about my own daughter's school, where the focus was also very much on the alphabet and phonics, even though she was only two years old.

As I researched the local school system in more detail, I looked at the myriad textbooks, workbooks, and exam papers used by Singaporean children. The reading process begins with phonics and basal readers, which are books with easy words and deliberate sound patterns; then, as children move up the academic ladder, the words they can sound out or decode get progressively harder: from "giggle" to "groan" to "gullible." Singaporean children get a lot of practice with phonics, spelling, reading comprehension, and writing. They memorize vocabulary words and fill in blanks in paragraphs with missing words. They underline verbs, circle subjects, and identify objects. They learn a formula for writing winning compositions; interestingly, many of the students and teachers I spoke with mentioned that certain topics—love, death, and rebellion, for example—are off-limits for students, particularly in elementary and middle school, as they would be looked on unfavorably by national examiners. From phonics to filling in the blanks to grammar exercises, I found that the meticulously organized, super-systematic Singaporean English curriculum rivals Singapore math for its sequencing, precision and ability to yield high scores on PISA exams. And as a result, many parents seem to encourage their kids to study English in much the same way as they encourage them to study math: through structured workbook exercises, drills, and games. However, while many of the parents I spoke with were conscious of raising their kids in a mathematical world, very few of the mothers I spoke with were consciously raising their kids in a world of books and stories.

The conversations I had with moms in Singapore made me realize (for the millionth time) that nothing about American approaches to parenting and education is universal. The bedtime reading ritual so firmly ensconced in American culture is not universally embraced by any means. And neither is the classroom read-aloud, or discussion about stories the teacher reads to the class. Lara, a Singaporean friend, confessed she was worried about her seven-year-old son's writing skills. "He's just not interested in writing, and his writing is of such poor quality. I'm quite concerned, but I'm not sure what to do. You're an English teacher. What do you suggest?" I gave her some easy suggestions to get him more interested in writing: he could write letters to his grandparents, write thank-you cards and birthday cards for friends and family, write a short story about his favorite superhero or sports star, or create a comic strip. I also emphasized the connection between reading and writing. Get him to read more for pleasure and he'll become a better writer. Laughing, she looked at me and said, "Those are really good suggestions. You know, I've been teaching him reading and writing in the same way as I teach math—through school readers, workbook exercises, and word games—but I think I need to reconsider this."

As Lara clearly articulated, many mothers in Singapore approach reading and writing in much the same way as they approach math. But here's the rub: Treating English like math doesn't make sense in the long run, because language and math are *not* the same creature. Consider the complex chasm between stories and simultaneous equations, between metaphors and multiplication. Think about the wide gulf between words and numbers, between the linear logic of geometric proofs and the whimsical suggestiveness of human conversations. Getting kids to become accomplished readers involves moving beyond the concrete and the literal, beneath the words on the page; it requires an immersion in stories and narratives, in feelings and fantasy, in subtext and suggestion. And to become good writers, kids need to read widely for pleasure and write in authentic and engaging contexts.

I couldn't help comparing approaches to reading and writing in America and Singapore, and the more conversations I had with mothers in Singapore, the more impressed I became with what Americans do when it comes to reading. In the US, I routinely encountered educators and parents who spoke with great passion about the power of immersing children in a language-rich environment and nurturing a deep love of reading in them. Now, I'm not saying that America's approach to reading is perfect by any means. It has lots of issues—the primary one being that kids from low-income schools and neighborhoods just don't get the kind of access to books, language, and stories that middle- and upper-class kids across the country do. But, overall, to make a large generalization, America has done an admirable job of creating **a national reading culture**. I think that it is America's emphasis on nurturing a love of reading in its children, from the very beginning of their lives all the way into adulthood, that makes American approaches to reading trump Asian approaches in the long run. The fact that heated public debates about the teaching of reading happen in America, the fact that there are educators who routinely argue that they've got to teach kids to *love* reading, the fact that parents feel so obligated to read books out loud to their young children on a daily basis: *that* is what makes America a reading culture.

While American educators and parents have long been involved in debates and discussions about how best to teach reading, a common cultural understanding seems to run through American discussions: reading is important *for its own sake*, reading is *pleasurable*, and the long-term goal of education is not just to teach a kid how to read, but to make sure that the kid will *want* to read on his or her own. I'm often reminded of Mark Twain's words, "The man who does not read has no real advantage over the man who cannot read." And it is, I would argue, the relative value of reading for pleasure that distinguishes America from Singapore and perhaps more largely from Asia.

THE READING WARS: Phonics and whole language

Interested in the varying approaches to early literacy, I began to look more closely at debates around early-childhood literacy not just in Singapore, but also in the US. Phonics study is central to reading instruction in Singapore, but is it the same in the US?

When I lived in America, I read many articles about the "reading wars" that pit the systematic study of phonics against a more organic exposure to the world of words and books, otherwise known as the "whole-language" approach. What were the outcomes of these debates? What was the history behind them?

Just as late twentieth-century reforms in math education moved the study of math away from algorithms, procedures, and math drills, twentieth-century reforms in language education moved the study of reading away from phonics, grammar, and punctuation. A generation of kids from the 1970s and '80s grew up without a systematic phonics approach and not much formal grammar; they were exposed to books and words and stories with the hope that they would "naturally" learn how to read. This approach sounds good at one level, but it had the unintended effect of leaving children without practical strategies for decoding unfamiliar language. While a small group of students—usually ones who have grown up in homes full of books—may be able to learn how to read through the whole-language approach, research indicates that most students need systematic and explicit instruction in letter sounds to make the cognitive leap required to read. On a side note, the same claim can be made for math: while more natural discovery-based methods might work for a small group of kids—usually kids who come from mathematical homes—the majority of kids need to be explicitly taught standard algorithms and procedures in order to gain strong math foundations. The math wars and the reading wars in the US are strikingly similar in many ways. In both English and math, kids were being asked to navigate a dense and tricky forest without a clear map; they needed to figure out a way to map the forest on their own. If it worked, then kids would have a superior understanding of the forest and the routes they had discovered; if it failed, however, kids would be left wandering around the forest, not knowing where they were going, defeated and lost.

By the time the '90s rolled around, a backlash had begun, and reading instruction became a hotly debated and politicized discussion, with American parents and politicians demanding a return to phonics. In fact, from 1990 to 1997, eighteen American states had one or more phonics bills introduced in legislative sessions; and by 1997, a total of thirty-three state legislators had passed bills that required schools to explicitly teach phonics.[11]

Phonics has now seen a resurgence in classrooms across the US, and most American literacy experts have found a comfortable place that includes elements of both "whole language" and "phonics instruction." They call this "balanced literacy." Contemporary education wisdom indicates that kids should experience *both* a systematic phonics instruction program *and* a whole-language-style immersion in stories, books, and language. The study of phonics gives kids the maps they need to decode individual words, while a whole-language approach encourages them to use a wide range of routes and really get to know the forest of sounds, words, and meaning, thereby giving them a much wider variety of skills to make sense of words on the page. More importantly, read-alouds, book discussions, and creative activities related to books and stories teach kids that books are interesting and reading is pleasurable.

---

11   James S. Kim, "Research and the Reading Wars," in *When Research Matters,* ed. Fredrick M. Hess (Cambridge, MA: Harvard University Press, 2008): 89–111.

If kids get all these forms of instruction, in an ideal world, they not only learn how to read but also develop an appreciation for reading.

VOCABULARY ACQUISITION: What's in a word?

While phonics is central to early reading instruction in Singapore, "word study" is central to the acquisition of vocabulary, particularly in the form of fill-in-the-blank-style exercises. Is explicit vocabulary instruction and memorization the best way to aid vocabulary acquisition? Or is an American-style "reading culture" the key to ensuring that children develop rich and wide-ranging vocabularies? And why is vocabulary acquisition so important, anyway?

Research indicates that the size of a child's vocabulary correlates significantly not only with reading outcomes, but also with IQ. Yale professor Robert Sternberg writes, "Vocabulary is probably the best single indicator of a person's overall intelligence. Stated in another way, if one wants a quick and not too dirty measure of a person's psychometrically measured intelligence, and thus has time to give just one brief test of it, vocabulary is generally the best predictor of overall score on a psychometric IQ test."[12]

I would add that a person's vocabulary is also deeply connected to their ability to think. In many ways, our thoughts are constrained by a lack of vocabulary but liberated by a rich and varied vocabulary. In his chilling novel *1984*, George Orwell reminded us that the destruction of words "narrows the range of our thoughts"; while a proliferation of words, with all their "shades of meaning," enlarges them. Having the right words helps us to clarify, organize, articulate, and understand our thoughts. The greater our vocabularies, the more sophisticated and complex our thoughts can be. And then these words allow us to communicate and share our thoughts with the outside world.

---

12 Robert Sternberg, "Three Basic Facts about Vocabulary," in *The Nature of Vocabulary Acquisition*, eds. Margaret G. McKeown and Mary E. Curtis (New York: Psychology Press, 2014): 89.

Sternberg and other researchers argue that most vocabulary is learned in context, and the vocabulary one acquires from wide reading is always superior, both in size and retention, to isolated vocabulary items a child memorizes for structured vocabulary exercises or assessments. The many benefits of wide reading include not only the development of a rich vocabulary but also an appreciation of the power of words. A staggering statistic: the average schoolchild acquires between 2,500 and 3,000 new words each year. Clearly, there is no way that a child could actively study, memorize, and retain this many words in a year. Most of these words, obviously, are learned incidentally, either because a child hears them used in context or reads them in context. Children who read a lot learn even more words. According to a 1992 study, children who read widely learn an average of 4,000 to 12,000 new words each year as a result of their reading.[13]

The most famous American study of vocabulary acquisition, the Hart and Risley study, compared the number of words that children of middle-class parents heard before age five with the number of words that impoverished children heard before age five. The study found that children from poor backgrounds or "language-impoverished homes" heard 32 million fewer words than their middle class peers.[14] This massive inequity means wealthier children enter school with a huge head start, and studies show that it is virtually impossible for impoverished children to narrow or close the gap. If anything, the gap widens each year, since children who already have good vocabularies tend to be more successful in school. This causes them to read and learn more, which then causes them to do even better academically. Educators refer to this as the "Matthew Effect," after the Bible verse found in the Gospel of Matthew: "For whosoever

---

13   Richard C. Anderson and William Nagy, "The Vocabulary Conundrum," in *The Professional Journal of the American Federation of Teachers* 16, no. 4 (1992).

14   Betty Hart and Todd Risley, *Meaningful Differences in the Everyday Experience of Young American children* (Baltimore, MD: Paul H. Brookes, 1995).

hath, to him shall be given, and he shall have more abundance: but whosoever hath not, from him shall be taken away even that he hath." In other words, the rich get richer in academic terms. In contrast, students who begin school behind the curve fall further and further behind over the years. In fact, *Time* magazine writer Annie Paul Murphy reported that one can accurately predict a child's future academic outcomes by third grade.[15] Numerous research studies, including the well-publicized study titled "Early Warning Confirmed" by the Annie E. Casey Foundation,[16] have confirmed the importance of third grade as a particularly important year. If a child is strong in reading and math in third grade, then he will do well throughout school. Kids who are unable to keep up in third grade tend to lag further and further behind throughout their school years. That's the Matthew Effect at work, with students who have strong skills in the early years getting better over time while those with weaker skills fall further behind.

What are the best ways to help children acquire vocabulary? While explicit teaching of vocabulary words can be helpful (especially if a student is studying for a test or an exam like the SAT), learning words in context is always preferable to learning words in isolation. When a student merely memorizes a vocabulary word, he may be able to define the word but he may not understand it well enough to use it effectively. In my experience, when students memorize vocabulary words from a textbook or worksheet, they don't fully *get* the word; they don't get all the connotations, all the baggage that the word carries, until they hear or read the word used in context often. While students in Singapore may "learn" a number of words through comprehension exercises, fill-in-the-blank worksheets, and other structured vocabulary exercises, these

15 Annie Paul Murphy "Why Third Grade is So Important: The Matthew Effect," *Ideas* (*Time* magazine's blog), September 26, 2012, http://ideas.time.com/2012/09/26/why-third-grade-is-so-important-the-matthew-effect/.

16 The Annie E. Casey Foundation. *Early Warning Confirmed*. Baltimore: The Annie E. Casey Foundation, 2013. http://www.aecf.org/resources/early-warning-confirmed/.

words will never be able to compete with those whose meanings are internalized through extensive independent reading. The cultivation of an independent reading life—of a lifelong habit of reading for pleasure—is the best way to help children gain not only a deep contextual understanding of words, but also an appreciation of the power, beauty, and nuance of words. Singaporean schools are beginning to emphasize reading for pleasure in their curricula, but because of the exam system that begins early in elementary school, the focus is invariably on what can be tested, not on the untestable and nonstandard act of independent reading.

In contrast, American educators who are less constrained by high-stakes national tests have the luxury of emphasizing independent reading through programs such as DEAR (Drop Everything and Read) and Readers' Workshop, a widely used reading program developed by Teachers College, Columbia University, that emphasizes encouraging children to read independently for pleasure. Furthermore, while parents in Singapore often marginalize reading for pleasure because it doesn't help children on their tests and exams, parents in the US are often urged to make read-alouds and independent reading a central part of the homework routine in the early years.

So what should a parent do? Numerous studies show a strong correlation between the number of books in the home and a child's reading and learning outcomes.[17] Additionally, research suggests that access to well-stocked libraries have a significant effect on the amount a child reads.[18] Clearly, public libraries and school libraries are absolutely crucial to fostering wide-ranging reading habits. One

---

17 Jeff McQuillan and Victoria Rodrigo, "Literature-based Programs for First Language Development: Giving Native Bilinguals Access to Books," in *Literacy Access, and Libraries Among the Language Minority Population*, ed. R. Constantino (Lanham, MD: Scarecrow, 1998): 209–224. James S. Kim, "Summer Reading and the Ethnic Achievement Gap," paper presented at the American Educational Research Association, Chicago, April 21, 2003.

18 Francisco Ramos and Stephen Krashen, "The impact of one trip to the public library: Making books available may be the best incentive for reading." *The Reading Teacher* 51, no. 7 (1998): 614–615.

American study found a strong relationship between the number of books per student in the school library and students' performance on a statewide reading test.[19] Every school should invest in its libraries. If your child attends a school that doesn't have a well-stocked library, you could organize the parents' association and raise money to create one. Lobby the administration and remind them of the enormous effect that school libraries have on student reading and learning outcomes.

I often see ads for expensive new international schools in Asia, and they all advertise their impressive facilities: swimming pools, playing fields, and computer labs. As a parent and educator, I always wonder why they never advertise the size and quality of their libraries. Of all the facilities in a school, the library, I would argue, is the most important. At the very heart of any excellent school should be an inviting library full of books and quiet spaces for thought, knowledge, learning, and intellectual exploration.

READING WITH MY SON: From America to Singapore

My own firsthand experience of America's love affair with childhood reading began when I took my newborn son to visit his pediatrician for a routine checkup. Hands full of baby paraphernalia—an overflowing diaper bag, a baby blanket, and a squalling baby—my husband and I arrived at the Dartmouth Hitchcock Hospital in New Hampshire, harried and flustered. Our sleepy, cranky baby was due for his six-month wellness visit. The pediatrician, a young and amiable man, quieted our son by distracting him with a hand puppet, and proceeded to ask us a number of questions about his development. He then fished out a basket of baby board books and asked us to choose one for our son. "Go ahead, take one. We want all our kids to enjoy books, so every baby gets one," he said, smiling. I picked out a book titled *What Do You Love?* by Jonathon London and began

---

19 Stephen Krashen, "School Libraries, Public Libraries, and the NAEP Reading Scores." *School Library Media Quarterly* 23 (1995): 235–238.

flipping through the pages. Meanwhile, our pediatrician jabbed our son with a number of needles, vaccinating him for a whole host of illnesses. I cringed as my son began to wail loudly.

When I left the hospital, I was preoccupied with my baby's cries and worried that he would experience side effects from that huge cocktail of vaccinations. It was only days later that I picked up *What Do You Love?* and began reading it aloud to my son. As I read the gentle rhyming words in the book, I thought about what the hospital was doing for its youngest patients. Books, I thought, are a type of vaccination too. *What Do You Love?* soon became one of my son's favorite books; as he grew older, he chewed on the book, played with it, gazed at it, and smiled at it. He loved cuddling up with me and listening to me read the words to him. I loved that book, too.

My husband graduated from business school at Dartmouth, so we left New Hampshire and moved to New York City, full of excitement and anxiety about working and raising children in the most vibrant city in the world. From age three to age four my son attended a warm and nurturing play-based preschool. The children were not explicitly taught how to read at this school; they sang songs about the alphabet and the sounds that each letter made, but most of their literacy instruction involved read-aloud sessions. Teachers would take small groups of children into a corner of the classroom and read a book out loud to them. The children, gathered around the teacher, would examine the pictures carefully and listen to the rhythms and sounds of the words. Then all the kids would talk about the book: What did they like about it? Did the characters do the right thing or not? Why did they do it? Their responses were three- and four-year-old responses; sometimes they made no sense at all, and the teachers would smile benignly and nod, but at other times the responses were thoughtful, and the teachers would cheer the children on with words of validation and praise. In their little voices, with their own innocent and limited understanding of the world, the children would actively engage with the book and discuss it.

While my son was not taught to sound out words at his preschool, he was intensely interested in stories. At preschool each morning, he would hear exuberant stories about families going on bear hunts and snails riding on whales. At home every evening, he and I would snuggle up together and read our favorite books over and over again while he focused intently on the pictures, characters, and plots. He particularly loved *Owl Moon*, a beautiful, poetic book about a young girl who goes into the forest on a winter's night to look for an owl. Although he didn't understand the meaning of all the words in the book, he was fascinated by the pictures, and drawn in by the rhythm and poetry of the language.

When my son was four and a half and my daughter was just ten months old, we packed up and left New York for Singapore. Soon after we arrived, I found myself treading carefully through difficult terrain when it came to my views on reading. In conversations with other moms in Singapore, I found myself often feeling defensive about my son's reading skills (or lack thereof). I realized that most mothers' primary concern was whether or not their children could sound out words. Could their preschool-aged children make the leap from sounding out the letters *c*, *a*, and *t* to reading the word *cat*? My son was nowhere near making this tremendous cognitive leap. He could sound out each individual letter, but he couldn't put them together and read them as a single word.

At first this didn't worry me at all. The American books that I read all said that kids will learn to read around age six, but here in Asia, mothers seemed to be panicking when their children couldn't read words by ages four or five. Additionally, Singaporean and Indian preschools gave little importance to reading aloud to children and discussing stories, often focusing almost exclusively on phonics instruction and sounding out words and reading simple sentences to get students ready for Primary 1 (first grade). I would often hear statements like, "My girl is already four but she can't read at all. I'm tearing my hair out. What am I to do?" or (with great pride) "My son is not even five, but he's already reading Level 4 readers." When I asked parents what they read to their children, they often pointed to reading primers: Ladybird readers and Oxford readers with simple words that the kids could read, rather than the wonderful fantasy worlds I was exploring with my son.

When I talked with other moms in Singapore, I began to feel reading was not really about books and stories and making meaning; it seemed instead to be merely about sounding out words. I often felt that the mothers around me were thinking about the acquisition of reading skills as an anxiety-arousing 100-meter sprint—something done quickly and intensely in order to hit an imaginary finish line. In contrast, as an English teacher and an avid reader myself, I had always thought of reading acquisition more like a long and beautiful hike through the woods—a trip that is, first and foremost, beautiful in its own right, full of images, sounds, and stories. Furthermore, in my mind, becoming a reader is not something that stops once a child hits a certain level with basic readers. It's an ongoing process: a high-school student is a far more sophisticated reader than an elementary-school student, even if both can decode words fairly easily. I was often surprised at the way many parents I encountered disregarded the longer-term goal of raising a child to cherish books and love reading, and instead prioritized the short-term goal of decoding words faster than the other children around. Parental anxiety, however, is a highly contagious disease, far worse than the common cold or the flu. I, too, began to feel anxious, and my focus began to shift from the celebration and enjoyment of books and stories to sounding out letters and reading words.

Now, I'm not marginalizing the importance of teaching students to decode words by sounding them out. All I'm saying is that this strategy is only one part of teaching students to read. Learning to sound out words is not an easy or unimportant task, and it is crucial that all kids—regardless of their backgrounds and their access to books—get this kind of instruction. When I worked in Baltimore as part of the Teach For America program, I did, in fact, have some students in eighth grade who had no practical strategies for decoding unfamiliar words. Similarly, when I volunteered at a community center for low-income students in Singapore, I had a couple of elementary-school students who were unable to sound out letters when trying to make sense of text—they relied on memory and guesswork instead. I fully understand why whole-language approaches to reading may not work for all kids in the context of a classroom, and the research about the importance of phonics instruction is unequivocal.

Eventually, my son learned to read, as most children do. In fact, the vast majority of students I have worked with arrive in high school able to sound out words with ease. Even my dyslexic students, who struggled far more with the process of decoding than their peers did, arrived in high school with the ability to read words. My own experiences as a high-school English teacher in a range of environments have convinced me that most schools and parents in America and Asia do a very good job of teaching students how to decode words.

The gaps, as I see them, have much less to do with decoding and much more to do with enjoying reading, understanding words, and constructing meaning. I have often encountered teenagers who dislike reading, and I have also worked with many students who don't fully understand what they read. They can decode the words with ease, but they don't know what the words mean. They can read a story, but they can't think about it and make inferences about it. They stay at the surface of the text, missing the pearls hidden in the oysters, blind to the layers of meaning beneath the words. Perhaps when parents marginalize the enjoyment and pleasure of reading and words in their single-minded desire to make their children learn to decode words and complete comprehension exercises, they unwittingly hurt the kids in the long run.

While American parents can learn many lessons from Asian approaches to math education, one of America's great strengths, I think, is that it celebrates children's literature and encourages parents to read to their children on a daily basis. The message that parents should read to their children for pleasure, and that making reading a lifelong habit is important, is woven deeply into the fabric of American culture in a way that it isn't in most Asian nations.

Public messages about the importance of reading to children are everywhere—from pediatricians who give away books to their infant patients to articles in the newspaper and public messages about reading on the subway. The "bedtime story" is a ritual firmly ensconced in American culture. In classrooms across the country, teachers spend a lot of time reading aloud to children, engaging children in discussions of books, and encouraging students to develop a lifelong love of reading. According to Wikipedia, the US published 309,957 new books in 2012, more than any other country in the world. Additionally, the world of children's and young-adult literature is overwhelmingly dominated by American writing; no country publishes as much for children and teens as the US does. While televisions, handheld electronics, and computers may be challenging and eroding America's book culture, I think that America still does an admirable job of promoting reading in schools and homes.

READING IN ASIA: What parents say

While it seems clear to me that in general America has done a much better job of creating a "reading culture" than most Asian nations

ASIAN PARENTS SPEAK OUT

"I let my daughters read whatever they want"

"The teachers at my daughter's school told us parents to restrict our children's reading choices. For example, they said that books such as Geronimo Stiltons often teach young children inappropriate things or words. Yet, up until now, I've been quite relaxed about letting my daughters read whatever they want. I throw all kinds of books at them— if they want to read the same book over and over again, that's fine with me. And we have a 'no TV' rule during the week. Many of my friends are surprised at how well my daughter does on her school compositions, and they ask me what my secret is…what workbooks and strategies I'm using to teach her how to score well on her compositions. I always answer truthfully that I just let her read a lot."

—**Faith Lee**, mother of Sophia (eight) and Lily (six)

have, I've found myself increasingly intrigued by the wide range of attitudes towards reading that I encounter among Asian parents and educators in Singapore. Over the last four years, I have discussed reading with a number of Asian mothers in Singapore, and, at least on the surface, they universally acknowledge its importance. I know many Indian and Chinese mothers who are avid readers themselves, and they do everything they can to inculcate a deep love of reading and stories in their children.

Lily, a Chinese-Singaporean mother, surrounded her sons with books and read aloud to them well into their teenage years. They read and discussed books together as a family, and unsurprisingly, her son (one of my students) was a voracious reader and a talented writer. "I'm so delighted that he's such a bookworm," she said at a parent-teacher meeting.

Another parent, Vikram, whose eight-year old daughter attends a local Singaporean school, said wistfully, "For my daughter, English classes seem to revolve around grammar instruction and fill-in-the-blank exercises. While I have no doubt that this is important, I wish so much that her teacher would engage her in rich and open-ended discussions of literature. My daughter loves reading; but reading, it seems, has nothing to do with school. Her reading interests are entirely separate and distinct from what happens in school because her English classes have very little to do with books, stories, and ideas."

Shanaz, a slender and intense Pakistani mother, attributed her daughter's love of reading to the reading culture that she created in her home. "We cherish the arts in our home," she said. "From poetry by Rumi and Ghalib to Western classics by Dickens and Bronte, we read and relish them all."

When I work with students who are strong writers, avid readers, and good critical thinkers, I assume that they must come from families that encourage and celebrate reading. I have met many Asian mothers and fathers who value reading tremendously, but there are also parents who seem to harbor a certain ambivalence toward it.

I met Lina, a fashionable mother from Delhi, at a Diwali party a year after moving to Singapore. She and her family had relocated to Singapore from Delhi in 2007, and her children attended an international school. As we talked about children, parenting, and schools, Lina mentioned that her daughter wasn't driven enough. "She's not ambitious or motivated," she said anxiously. "She spends all her time reading novels. I keep telling her to at least read nonfiction. That way she'll learn something. Or I try to make her do more math and science. But no, she just wants to read."

In another interview with a Chinese mother, I encountered a certain fear and hesitancy towards reading. "I speak Mandarin at home, and I'm not an avid reader myself. I would like my son to read more, but since I can't help him, I'm not sure what to do. One summer, I bought some English classics for him to read and tried to make him read the books every day, but it didn't work. He read for a little while and then said he didn't understand the books. I think that he will never be strong in English. Math and science are his strengths; those are the subjects he can score well in, so I encourage him in those areas. Let him develop his strengths." When I asked her whether he read in Mandarin, she looked surprised, and replied, "Only for his Chinese classes."

At a meeting with two earnest South Indian parents, I mentioned that their son should read more for pleasure to develop his vocabulary and his intuitive understanding of grammar and syntax. Though he was fluent in English and considered it his first language, his sentences were often awkwardly constructed and his vocabulary was limited. "Yes, yes, he should read more. My son is a typical Indian boy, you know, good at math and science, but not very interested in reading," responded the father with a nervous laugh.

Another anxious Singaporean mother told me, "I buy books to read for my daughter, but I think what really helps her are worksheets on vocabulary, grammar, and composition. I make her memorize vocabulary and complete worksheets. I think that will help her with her school assignments more than reading. Also, I can see the progress she makes. With reading, I never know if she really is making any progress at all—it's very hard to see real progress when children just read for fun."

Another Chinese mother, originally from Hong Kong, who over the years has become a close friend of mine, remarked, "The problem with Chinese kids is that they don't think about reading books at all. Books are to be studied for exams, but the concept of reading for pleasure hasn't really taken off in Asia." (Ironically, this particular mom is an avid reader herself, as is her middle-school-aged son.)

EXPLORING THE ROOTS OF THE READING ISSUE: Why the ambivalence?

As all these discussions indicate, some Asian parents are ambivalent at best, or nervous and insecure at worst, about their children's attitudes towards reading. Is this because English is still a second language for so many Asian children in Singapore? For them, the language of the home—of comfort, affection, and family—is still Hindi, Tamil, Mandarin, Hokkien, Malay, or some other Asian language. English is a formal language reserved for the outside world. As a result of Singapore's colonial legacy, English is the official language of the island, but it is often *not* the language that mothers associate with love and emotion; rather, it is associated with work and the public sphere. I often wonder about the high psychological costs that countries and societies experience when they replace their own languages with the language of the colonizer, the language of power. What is lost in this process of linguistic displacement? Like refugees, people and societies who are exiled from their own ancestral language and literary heritage lose a part of themselves. This reality about language, which is true not just in Singapore but also in India and most other former British colonies, can cause mothers to feel somewhat intimidated or insecure about the role of English in their children's lives. Immigrants in the US may experience a similarly ambivalent emotional reaction to English.

Research suggests that mothers who talk to and read to their children often, **regardless of the language they use**, provide an essential cognitive and linguistic foundation for all later learning across all subject areas. In other words, a child who is read to in Mandarin, Japanese, Hindi, French, or Spanish will have the cognitive and linguistic foundation to thrive in an English class down the road.[20] For bilingual families living in English-speaking countries, parents may feel it's advantageous to encourage their children to acquire English at the expense of the mother tongue, but maintaining and developing the home language through conversation, storytelling, and read-alouds will enhance a child's development in both languages. In fact, if anything it will ensure that the child holds on to her home language and culture, giving her the gift of bilingualism. Parents should *always* share their love of reading in their own language with their children. For a twenty-first century child who attends a school where everyone speaks English, a love of reading in the home language will eventually translate into a love of reading in English.

One issue that arises, however, is that while most Asian cultures have a rich oral tradition, with lots of stories and myths that are handed down from one generation to the next in the mother tongue, they unfortunately do not have anywhere near the number of children's books that the West does. For example, when I was trying to teach my children Hindi, I had to look very hard to find children's storybooks published in that language. Similarly, Chinese and Malay parents in Singapore say that the number and range of children's books available in their mother tongues is tiny compared to what is available in English. In Singapore's public libraries, the Chinese section is significantly smaller than the English section, and the Malay and Tamil sections are almost nonexistent. Most Asians in Singapore are bilingual, but their reading lives are almost completely in English.

One of the byproducts of the language issue is that kids who read in English are overwhelmingly exposed to children's books

---

20 Maryanne Wolf, *Proust and the Squid: The Story and Science of the Reading Brain* (New York: Harper Collins, 2007): 106.

about white American or British kids in Western contexts. This raises a host of issues related to values, culture, and identity. Some of the parents I spoke with bemoaned the values and characters that their children encounter in English-language books, saying that many of them teach American values that sharply contradict Asian mores. One parent, for example, criticized *Diary of a Wimpy Kid*, saying that it taught his young son to be disrespectful and talk back to his parents.

As a parent myself, I worry that my children don't encounter enough characters who look and sound like them. When my young daughter makes up stories that have Western protagonists with blond hair and blue eyes, I worry that all the Western children's literature that she reads, along with the Western media she consumes, has somehow distorted her sense of self; why, I wonder, doesn't she make up stories with Indian protagonists who look like her? To counter my worries, I make sure that I read a wide range of stories from around the world to my kids, and when I tell my young daughter stories, the protagonists tend to be strong Indian girls (like her) who have chocolate-brown skin, long black hair, and names like Sarita or Rohini. While I love Western children's literature, it is important to me that my children see themselves in at least some of the literature they read so they know that their stories matter just as much as that of their white Western peers. In addition to Indian children's literature, I also actively look for books with East Asian protagonists, black protagonists, and other non-typical protagonists so that my kids realize that everyone has a story to tell, and all our stories matter.

Ken, a Chinese-Singaporean friend of mine, eloquently captured the issues that many Asian kids reading in English face when he described his own childhood reading experiences. "I loved American and British books when I was growing up, and I saw myself in those books, but I always saw myself as a white boy eating Western foods. My forays into literature as a child had nothing to do with the reality of my life as a young Singaporean boy who stood up to greet teachers and elders, who knew only tropical sun and rain, and who ate chicken rice and *ban-mian*." I thought about this recently as I graded my high-school students' short stories; interestingly, my Asian students almost always write short stories with white protagonists in American or European settings, again raising questions about the effects of an Asian childhood dominated by Western children's literature.

But the lack of fluency or comfort with English and the overwhelming Western context of children's literature in English are not the only reason that Asian parents I encountered expressed hesitation or ambivalence about reading. Some Asian mothers, partly because of their own anxiety about their children's futures, tend to devalue the reading experience because literature is a "subject where it's hard to score high marks." Some parents saw reading as an indulgence because it doesn't lead directly to lucrative STEM careers. Others dismissed free reading because it doesn't produce tangible, measurable results. Like playing, daydreaming, and painting, the learning that occurs while reading a book for pleasure is hard to quantify and describe. Yet, there are numerous studies that show that the cognitive gains reading provides are real.[21] Reading helps children develop not only their vocabulary but also their intuitive understanding of the way language works. Students who read develop an ear for language—they can tell what sounds right or looks right, and what doesn't. They begin to play with sentence structures and combine ideas in interesting and nuanced ways. Studies even show that reading literary fiction helps students develop better interpersonal skills; researchers found that reading a piece by Chekhov or Munroe helped subjects read facial expressions and body language better.[22]

The idea that reading is somehow less important than math and science, however, seems deeply embedded in the Asian psyche, though it is starting to change as parents realize that language and

---

21 Stephen D. Krashen, *The Power of Reading: Insights from the Research* (Westport, CT: Libraries Unlimited, 2004): 35–38.

22 David Comer Kidd and Emanuele Castano, "Reading Literary Fiction Improves Theory of Mind," *Science* 342 (October 2013): 377–380.

communication are crucial to success in a highly globalized and interconnected world. While math may appeal more to parents because it is easily measurable and it seems more explicitly connected to lucrative careers, the twenty-first century demands constant written and spoken communication, and the lingua franca of the internet and the modern world, for better or for worse, happens to be English. Students have to be able to read, write, and speak well. And the best way to make sure this happens, in fact the *only* way to make sure this happens, is to make sure your child reads.

READING MAGIC

For practical data-driven parents, there's a lot of hard scientific evidence that shows how beneficial story books are for children. Reading for pleasure by children has been studied in great detail, and every study reveals a very high correlation between reading, intelligence, and academic success. Here is what the research says:[23]

- Reading makes kids smarter and more knowledgeable.
- When children read, they become better readers and writers.
- Reading helps children learn grammar, syntax, and punctuation.
- Through reading, children begin to develop an intuitive understanding of how language works, and they begin to realize when a sentence sounds right and when it doesn't.
- Reading helps children develop their vocabularies, and multiple studies show a high correlation between the size of a person's vocabulary and their IQ.
- Reading helps children learn about their world; books introduce children to a range of geographical and cultural settings, to scientific knowledge, and to history.
- Reading frees the imagination. A child can fly through the air

---

23 Cunningham and Stanovich, "Early reading acquisition and its relation to reading experience and ability 10 years later," 934–45.
Stanovich, West, and Harrison, "Knowledge growth and maintenance across the life span: The role of print exposure," 811–826.
Krashen, *The Power of Reading: Insights from the Research*.

with superheroes and save the world, or climb a tree and enter a magical land. Anything becomes possible in a book.

- Reading helps children develop concentration and extend their attention spans. Since reading requires substantial mental energy, it engages the brain fully and literally makes our children smarter.

So that's quite a list, isn't it? But here's the catch: The real reason that a child should read has nothing to do with practicality. It has nothing to do with numbers, data, or studies about IQ and vocabulary size. The real reason that a child should read has everything to do with imagination, creativity, beauty, empathy, and pleasure. The real reason that a child should read is that good books are magical.

Like carefully guarded keys, books open mysterious doors to rooms full of treasures; they allow us to travel in time—back into the past, far into a distant future. Through books, we travel across oceans and centuries to places and times we would never otherwise encounter. And through books, we travel deep into our own minds and hearts, as well as the minds and hearts of others.

Books, stories, and poetry are part of our shared humanity; they help us understand and make sense of the human experience. Across time and place, in a wide range of languages, humans have been telling stories, crafting poems, singing songs, and expressing their deepest feelings and fears through the spoken and written word. While our technologies and lifestyles may have changed unrecognizably over the last millennia, the words of Kabir and Kalidas, Li Bai and Cao Xueqin, Milton and Shakespeare still resonate today—a broken heart then is not unlike a broken heart now, and the ache and longing of love a thousand years ago is much the same as the ache and longing of love today.

I have so many memories of intense and moving reading experiences as a child and a teenager. I remember clearly my induction into the world of readers. One hot summer in Chennai, when I was almost seven years old, the sun filtered through the leaves of the mango tree outside our house and glinted off the pages of my book. I sat with my back against the trunk of the tree, reading each page with studied concentration. I held my breath, my heart pounding in my chest, as I wondered whether or not Joe, Beth, and Frannie would ever escape from the clutches of Dame Snap. The children had climbed up the ladder to one of the magical lands at the top of the Faraway Tree, and they had, unfortunately, gotten trapped in a terrible land. Would they find their way out? Every day that summer, I retreated to the shade of the mango tree and read. Every night, I fell asleep dreaming about magical lands and fantastical adventures. By the end of my summer vacation, I had finished reading *The Folk of the Faraway Tree*, my first chapter book, and I had become a reader.

Now, as a parent and teacher, I feel a sense of deja vu as I watch my own children and students enter the world of books and stories. When my eight-year-old son laughs out loud as he reads about the terrible fate of Augustus Gloop, that "big fat nincompoop" in Roald Dahl's *Charlie and the Chocolate Factory*, I am reminded of the humor and laughter of childhood reading. When my five-year-old daughter begs me to read her one more chapter from *Charlotte's Web*, I am reminded of the way books draw us into their worlds, urging us to imagine all kinds of possibilities. And when one of my ninth graders clutches *The Kite Runner* tightly in his hands and tells me that he has never loved a book so much, I am reminded again of the power of books and words to move us, literally, to tears.

There are plenty of reasons for parents to surround their children with books and provide them with the space and time to read, read, read. When you see your son or daughter curled up in bed with a book, don't dismiss it as a waste of time. That time is precious. Your child is learning more than you know.

TIPS FOR PARENTS HOW TO BUILD A LANGUAGE-RICH HOME

- **Surround your child with good books**. Buy or borrow lots of books for your child, and choose them as deliberately as possible. While e-books are wonderful, they are no substitute for physical books, especially for children. It is important to have lots of physical books around, because a child who is bored will often pick up a book he finds on a shelf to read. In contrast, a child with an iPad will probably end up playing a game rather than browsing a virtual bookshelf to find an e-book.

- **Create a good book collection for yourself and your home**, and make sure you model good reading habits. Having books in the home sends a powerful signal to your children about what you value. If you have bookshelves full of books, and if you read on a regular basis, your children will know that you value reading and that you are a reading family. Many studies show a high correlation between books in the home and reading outcomes of children.

- **If your mother tongue is a language other than English, share your language with your children**: Read to them in Mandarin or Hindi or Spanish or whatever language you speak at home. Provide them books in both English and your home language, but also share your love of reading by reading to them in your first language.

- **Become a member of a library**. Find a public or private library and take your child there on a regular basis. Encourage your child's school to build up its library collection; have parents donate money and books to the school library.

- **Read to your children on a daily basis**. When they are young—from six months onwards—introduce them to the magic of words by telling them stories and reading them picture books. Read with as much emotion and energy as you can. Cuddle up together and read; reading together is a wonderful bonding exercise.

- **As your children grow up, continue to read aloud to them**. A child's listening age is usually a few years ahead of her reading age, so she will be able to listen to more challenging stories than she will be able to read independently. When I was twelve years old, my mother read *To Kill A Mockingbird* out loud to my sister and me, a couple of chapters every night. I loved that experience, and I remember it vividly.

■ **As you read to your children, ask open-ended questions**: Why do you think the character did that? Would you have done the same thing? Was the character's decision right or wrong? What does this story tell us about friendship? Or about truth or justice? Did you like the book? Why or why not? This technique, called "dialogic reading," helps children learn to process and analyze what they read. Don't expect a "right" answer; instead be open to your child's interpretations and thoughts. The idea of dialogic reading is to help your child think for himself and construct his own understanding of a text.

■ **When you read to your children, discuss words that they may not know or fully understand**. Then try to use those words in conversations with them to reinforce vocabulary learning. Children need to hear the same word used in context multiple times to really internalize its meaning. Also, use a rich vocabulary yourself. Don't dumb down your vocabulary for your children; instead, use more precise and nuanced words. As a teacher and a parent, I intentionally elevate the level of my vocabulary for the benefit of my students and my own children. For my own children, for example, I might use the word "subside" instead of stop. ("Oh look, the rain is subsiding. Now you can go play.") For my students, who are much older, I might use the word "ambiguous" instead of unclear. ("Yes, you're right, the character's motives seem somewhat ambiguous, don't they?")

■ **Take books for your children with you on vacations and trips**. If possible, find books that relate to the place you are visiting. For example, if you are visiting a game reserve, you may want to take nonfiction books on animals as well as fiction books that are set in forests (*The Jungle Books*, perhaps) or have animal characters. Similarly, if you are visiting a particular country or city, you might want to get your children some fiction and nonfiction books that are set in or around that city or country. Reading books about a place *before* you visit it will often help your child get excited about going, and it will make the trip more meaningful for the child.

■ **If your child is a reluctant reader, try to find books on subjects that she is interested in**. Sometimes getting a child hooked on books is just a matter of finding the right book for that particular child. If she loves science, look at science-fiction books or even nonfiction books. If she is a cricket fan, get her biographies of famous cricketers. If she is very relationship-oriented, look for books about families and friendships. Let her interests lead the way.

■ **When children are young, give them a mix of books**, both in terms of difficulty levels and in terms of genre, content, and subject matter. If your son loves *Beast Quest*, then go ahead and get him some of those books, even if you feel the series is formulaic, predictable, and not particularly well written. However, make sure that you also expose him to children's classics and to nonfiction. This is true for teens as well: they need a mix of easy and challenging reads, popular series and classics, fiction and nonfiction, prose and poetry.

■ **Buy books that are set in a wide range of cultural contexts**. Make sure your children have lots of books that reflect your own cultural context; for example, if you are Indian, make sure that they read literature about Indian children in Indian contexts. Also make sure that you expose them to other cultures than your own. Through literature, you can help your children learn about and empathize with people from around the world.

■ Since reading and writing are closely intertwined, if you **encourage your child to write and illustrate his own original stories or comic strips**, he may very well become excited about reading other people's stories. When your child writes for pleasure, don't worry too much about grammar and spelling. If you spend too much time correcting him, he may start to see writing as a chore. Also, an intense focus on grammar and spelling may inhibit his imagination. The goal initially is to cultivate a love of reading and writing. Once a child is excited about reading and writing stories, then you can focus more on the technical aspects of writing.

■ One thing that has worked well in my family is **time on the weekend for "family reading."** On a lazy Sunday afternoon, we all grab our books and read in the living room together. Sometimes during family meals we will go around the table, and each person will say what they've been reading and share their thoughts about the book with the family. These are informal book conversations, but they have helped my children internalize the idea that we are a reading family and that reading is central to our lives.

■ **Limit screen time**: One of the biggest reasons kids don't read is that they are spending their time on screens of some sort. Social media, video games, movies, and the internet give books a lot of competition. If you want your kids to read, limit their screen time and offer them books instead.

■ **Give your child time to read.** Many of my high-school students tell me they don't have time to read because they have so much homework and so many extracurricular activities. As a parent, you have to encourage your child to make time to read. If you see her curled up with a good book, don't disturb her and tell her that she needs to finish her math homework or her science project. While it may seem as though the opportunity cost of spending an afternoon reading is high, the opposite is actually true. The opportunity cost of *not* reading is very, very high.

■ **Pay it forward**: Donate books to school libraries and give books to children who may not have access to books. If possible, donate money to nongovernmental organizations like Room to Read, which provide low-income children with books and education (roomtoread.org). *All* children, rich and poor, should have access to books.

CHAPTER 3

Memorization, Practice, Exams, and Other Things That Asians Love

Singapore, October 2012

"I don't really care about facts," announced one of my Western colleagues emphatically. We were discussing curriculum and pedagogy in the faculty lounge. "Kids can look facts up on Google any time. Why do they need to waste time memorizing them?" she continued. "What we need to teach are higher-order thinking skills—we need to teach our students how to think."

I stayed quiet, trying to figure out where I stood in this debate that pitted factual knowledge against thinking skills.

Chennai, India, October 2012

Two of my friends, Mallika and Samaya, have sons in the same class at an Indian school in Chennai. One afternoon, as the three of us were chatting over tea at Mallika's house, the following conversation ensued:

Mallika: Has your son started preparing for the science test yet? There's so much to study!
Samaya: Yes, he's been studying hard. But there's way too much for a child of his age to memorize.

Mallika: I've been making my son read each paragraph and then write it in his own words so that he understands and remembers the information.

Samaya: His own words? No, no. I just make my son memorize it. God knows what he'll write down if he puts it in his own words. Much safer for him to memorize it properly.

I was struck by the contrast between my colleague's viewpoint and that of my Indian friends. They seemed to me to capture two ends of a wide spectrum of views on knowledge, content, and memorization. At one end of the spectrum are people who seem to believe that knowledge is unimportant. These twenty-first-century-skill enthusiasts believe that critical thinking can take place in a vacuum, and they pit knowledge and thinking against each other. Facts, memorization, textbooks, worksheets, and drills are all bad words in their lexicon. They believe that students should "think creatively and critically," but they don't believe that it is important for students to actually *know* anything.

At the other end of the spectrum are people who believe that memorization is so important that it supersedes understanding and thinking altogether. Conditioned by competitive exam systems, these parents and educators believe that memorizing content "word for word" is a good use of a child's time, because it will ostensibly result in high scores on high-stakes tests.

A HISTORY OF MEMORIZATION IN EDUCATION

For millennia, students around the world have been expected to memorize vast quantities of content, and this process has been the centerpiece of education. In ancient India, formal education focused largely on memorizing passages from Vedic texts and scriptures. Young Brahmin boys would spend hours committing religious scriptures to memory. Education and religion were inextricably linked, and the goal of both seemed to be the preservation of religious texts. In modern times, Indian students spend hours learning a great deal of information by heart, some of it of questionable worth. When I did my Grade 10 ICSE exams, I memorized vast quantities of information. Some of it has stayed with me after all these years; some of it has not.

In China, from the days of the famed imperial examination to the present-day Gaokao (college entrance exam), memorization has formed the centerpiece of education. Today, Chinese students spend hours memorizing model essays and vast quantities of factual information for brutally competitive high-stakes exams. A Chinese mother I interviewed told me about her nephew in China who studies from 8 a.m. to 11 p.m. every day, with only two breaks—an hour-long lunch break and time for an afternoon snack from 3:30

ASIAN PARENTS SPEAK OUT

"Laissez-faire parenting leaves too much to chance"

"I've thought a lot about the laissez-faire approach to parenting, and I finally decided that it just doesn't work. I used to be conflicted, because I would read Western articles, and then I would see the intense pressure that my Chinese and Korean colleagues were putting on their own children. I would see their focus on academics, particularly math and science, and see the results. So although this is something I used to worry about, I finally decided that laissez-faire parenting leaves too much to chance, and it just doesn't work. Especially not for our kids. Our kids have to be pushed, because Asia is not structurally at the same point as the West is. We still have a long way to go before we can confidently say that we have the same degree of infrastructure and opportunity as America. And one has to take into account the numbers—there are so many of us Asians! The fact of the matter is that our children have to compete more; they have to aim higher. So we've got to push our children hard. And you know what? Our kids can handle it. Also, if you want to excel at anything, you've got to work really, really hard. That's the way life is. There's also lots of satisfaction in hard work and competition. I personally love working hard."

—**Tarun**, father of Aalok (nine) and Dilip (seven)

to 4:30—as he prepares for the dreaded Gaokao. She described the way he memorizes whole model essays word for word (or character for character, given that we're talking about Chinese essays). In addition to regular classes during the week, high-school seniors in China have special classes on Saturdays, and can take only one week off in the summer and one week off for Chinese New Year. The rest of the year is devoted to studying, much of it involving memorization, drills, and practice.

Interestingly enough, in the West, too, up until the industrial revolution and the advent of mass schooling, education also involved huge amounts of memorization. A classical education required knowledge of Latin, which involved lots of rote memorization of Latin grammar and whole passages from classical literature. The first stage of the classical education undertaken by scholars like Shakespeare was grammar, which centered around memorization of factual knowledge and Latin texts. The subsequent stages included logic (the mechanics of analysis) and rhetoric (using language to instruct or persuade).

FROM THE ORAL TRADITION TO PRINT TO A DIGITAL WORLD: Do we still need memory?

Before mass literacy became the norm, people relied entirely on their memories to preserve and transmit information. Obviously, with the emergence of writing and reading, people depended far less on the spoken word for information, stories, and ideas. People didn't have to remember things anymore, because they could write them down and then refer to the written word.

In his philosophical work *Phaedrus*, Plato describes Socrates' fears as he watched the world around him transform from an oral society to a literate one. One of his worries was that in a literate world, people would begin relying on the written word, and in the process would lose their ability to memorize and remember. In some ways, perhaps, Socrates' fears did materialize. In his travel book *Nine Lives: In Search of the Sacred in Modern India*, William

Dalrymple examines the remnants of the oral tradition in India today and then asserts that literacy kills oral traditions. When people become literate, they lose their ability (or inclination? Or need?) to memorize and recite thousands of verses of poetry that have been transmitted orally from one generation to the next.[24]

When the world begins to change in revolutionary ways, much is gained, but much is also lost. Clearly, the written word brought tremendous benefits to our societies. It enabled us to communicate across distance and time. It allowed us access to far more information than we could ever commit to memory. And it made the preservation and acquisition of knowledge much easier. It also made knowledge far more accessible, thereby democratizing it in unheard-of ways. However, the newly literate world also saw the loss of a whole way of life. The written word doesn't have the same life and vibrancy as the spoken word does. When one speaks, communication is enhanced by physical tone of voice, intonation, gesture, and expression. There is something alive and warm about listening to a story or watching a play. There is a social element to the spoken word and the oral tradition that is lost when one engages in the solitary pleasure of a book. And of course, as so many thinkers and writers assert, when one begins to read and write, one stops committing words to memory.

I watched my own son "lose" his ability to memorize whole books as he became acquainted with the written word. As a preliterate toddler, he memorized his storybooks word for word because he still relied on his memory to access information and stories. Of course, at the time, I was convinced that he was a genius, but after a little research on the subject, I realized that this was very normal toddler behavior. However, as he slowly and painstakingly became literate, he no longer recited and remembered every word in his books. He relied much less on his memory, and as a result, his capacity to memorize seems to have rusted over time. Now, as a

---

24 William Dalrymple, *Nine Lives: In Search of the Sacred in Modern India* (New York: Vintage Books, 2009): 92

literate person, he can just look at the book and read the words; he doesn't need to remember them.

Does research support this idea that literacy kills or harms our memory? Apparently not. The French neuroscientist Stanislas Dehaene claims that the opposite is true. In his book *Reading in the Brain*, he cites a variety of experiments performed on literate and illiterate women in Portugal and concludes that the literate people had better memories. Dehaene writes, "Illiterates can remember the gist of stories and poems, but their verbal working memory–the temporary buffer that stores instructions, recipes, names or phone numbers over short periods of time–is vastly inferior to [that of literate people].[25] However, while there is no scientific evidence to suggest that literacy harms our *ability* to remember, there is tremendous evidence that it eliminates our *need* to remember. Writing simply removes the necessity of memorizing.

If literacy eliminates the need for memory, then what does technology do? With all our electronic gadgets, do we ever need to remember anything? When I teach now, I can look up pretty much anything instantaneously. As a kid, I used to remember people's phone numbers, but now there is no real need for me to do this. It's faster for me to retrieve a number from my cell-phone contact list than it is for me to retrieve the number from my memory. Phone numbers, historical dates, poems, mathematical formulae are all just a click away. And with the assurance that all this material exists outside us, safely stored in words and numbers on our various gadgets, we don't have to bother to remember anything. So, in a world where we are all electronically connected all the time, is memory totally and utterly redundant? We have our electronic memories; do we need our human memories at all?

With the huge shift from a print-based world to an electronic world, we are even less reliant on our memories than we used to be. Should educators make students memorize anything? Is there value in memorizing the multiplication tables? (After all, we have

25 Stanislas Dehaene, *Reading in the Brain* (Penguin Books, 1999): 208–210.

calculators.) Is there any value in memorizing a poem? Is there any value in memorizing historical dates and scientific facts? In schools around the world, teachers still make students do this kind of work on a routine basis. Kids have to memorize and recite poems and Shakespeare speeches. They have to memorize historical information and scientific facts. Are there benefits to committing information to memory? Should we be asking students to remember things for closed-book tests and exams, or should all our assessments be open-book and open-laptop evaluations? What is the connection between memorizing and learning? Does an English student benefit from memorizing a beautiful poem?

In the last two decades, educators around the world have challenged the role that memorization plays in education, arguing that in a digital world, memorization is not necessary, and accumulating information certainly shouldn't be the goal of an education. Yet this is obviously a huge shift in educational theory. For millennia, educators have demanded that students commit vast quantities of information to memory. Will memory really become an obsolete tool of the past?

MEMORIZATION: The good, the bad, and the ugly

Despite print literacy and Google, memorization, I would argue, is still valuable. In fact, research suggests that it is *very* valuable. Cognitive Scientist Daniel Willingham bucks the trend in the US by defending memorization and knowledge. In his book *Why Don't Students Like School?*—which actually has nothing to do with whether or not students like school and everything to do with how students learn—Willingham reminds parents and educators that students can only develop a deep understanding of a topic if they have already internalized sufficient background knowledge. Without a strong knowledge base, they won't be able to understand and analyze anything they read or see. They have to be able to fit new knowledge into some kind of preexisting framework for it to make sense. For example, when a student reads a newspaper article, he'll only understand what he's reading if he has some background knowledge on the topic. Newspaper articles assume that readers know quite a bit of history and politics, among other things. Young children find newspapers absolutely incomprehensible, primarily because they lack the knowledge base necessary to understand the articles. Similarly, it is very difficult to conduct meaningful research in any area without first knowing quite a bit of background information. Students need to have enough contextual knowledge to know what questions to ask, what to look for, and how to evaluate information. In any subject area, the more you know, the easier it is to comprehend new information. From a cognitive standpoint, facts are important, and a content-rich curriculum is vital.

In addition to supplying knowledge required for critical thinking, the process of memorizing information and transferring it from working memory to long-term memory has cognitive benefits. In his beautiful book *The Shallows*, Nicholas Carr asserts that memory is absolutely crucial to thinking. He writes:

"Scientific evidence suggests that as we build up our personal store of memories, our minds become sharper. The very act of remembering appears to modify the brain in a way that can make it easier to learn ideas and skills in the future. We don't constrain our mental powers when we store new long-term memories. We strengthen them. With each expansion of our memory comes an enlargement of our intelligence."[26]

So yes, memorization matters. We may have pens, books, calculators, and Google, but we still need our human memories. If we completely outsource our human memories to machines, we'll pay a high cognitive price.

Willingham's book seems to be directed at progressive Western educators who shun more traditional approaches to education in favor of new education trends: discovery-based math, reading and writing workshops, "flipped" classrooms, and technology-centric

---

26 Nicholas Carr, *The Shallows: What the Internet is Doing to Our Brains* (New York: W.W. Norton & Company, 2010): 192.

teaching. It reminds contemporary American educators that students still need to know factual information and they need to practice lots of basic skills.

But what about Asia? Have twenty-first-century Asian parents and educators abandoned their focus on memorization as well? In Western media, Asians tend to be stereotyped as expert memorizers who learn vast quantities of information by rote, and Asian systems are often denigrated as being too focused on memorization. In her book *Cultural Foundations of Learning*, education professor Jin Li[27] relates that one of her American professors at Harvard once told her, "All Chinese students do is rote learning!" Similarly, in many conversations with expatriates in Singapore, I have often heard the stereotype that Singapore schools and Singaporean families are focused only on rote learning and exam preparation. "They don't teach children to think independently," declared one British expat, who had just arrived in Singapore and had had no contact with locals whatsoever. In fact, despite the extraordinary scores and accolades that Singapore students earn on international tests, many expats—particularly Westerners—eschew the local system in favor of far more expensive international schools. When I ask parents at international schools why they decided against educating their children at a local Singaporean school, I often hear statements such as, "The local system is all about rote learning," or "Local kids are taught to follow rules, memorize information, and take tests, but they are not taught to think independently and express themselves creatively." How true are these stereotypes, I wondered?

In my conversations with Asian mothers in Singapore, I encountered some conflicting views on memorization. On the surface, Asian parents seem to agree with Western rhetoric about the uselessness of memorization: they, too, criticize "rote learning" and "mindless memory work," arguing that it is worthless in

---

27 Jin Li, *Cultural Foundations of Learning: East and West* (New York: Cambridge University Press, 2012): 72.

the twenty-first century. Yet as I probed more deeply, I found that most of the mothers maintained a sort of deep-seated reverence for "knowledge," which they believed must be memorized. In fact, most of them assumed that a child's education, almost by definition, must include memorizing substantial quantities of information.

Asian parents who have had an Asian education themselves but nonetheless choose to send their children to Western-style international schools are a particularly fascinating group, because they witness the differences between their children's Western education and their own Asian education on a daily basis. This causes them to constantly question their own paradigms, and also to impose their own experiences and conditioning onto the education that their children receive. I'm guessing that this may be true of immigrant parents in the US as well; they probably simultaneously appreciate the creativity of the American system and critique its lack of "exam-style rigor." The Asian parents I spoke with whose kids attended international schools expressed worries that their children were *not* memorizing enough information. On the one hand, they chose to send their children to international schools to escape the "rote learning" that they associate with Asian school systems, and they appreciate the projects and discussions that their kids engaged in at school. On the other hand, however, they often believe deep down that a substantial amount of memorization is very important. And they feel nervous and conflicted when they watch their children engage in an education system that is wholly unfamiliar to them. "These children don't study the way we did. They don't understand what it means to sit at a desk and study a textbook," said one mother earnestly.

"We Asians have a big advantage: we aren't afraid of making our children memorize a lot of information, from their times tables to vocabulary words to science facts," said another.

"Knowing facts is important and memory work is beneficial," insisted yet another mother, who worries that her young son doesn't ever have to memorize anything at his international school. She has made him memorize poems to sharpen his memory skills, arguing that the lack of "memorization" and "studying" is a real weakness of the school he attends.

These views didn't surprise me at all. As a teenager studying for my ICSE exams in India, I remember memorizing whole textbooks of information in the sciences and humanities. While my teachers were very committed and supportive professionals, the system forced them to think almost exclusively in terms of content that needed to be memorized. They spoke the language of national exams: "covering portions," "completing the syllabus," and endless "revisions." When I talk to my Indian students who have come directly from Indian schools in India, they assure me that nothing has changed. "We were expected to memorize so much information," they say emphatically. "Our education revolved around memorizing textbooks, and we were rarely asked to think independently or interpret a text on our own. The exams were all about regurgitating the right answer, and the teachers believed that there was just one correct interpretation of every poem or novel. We were never asked what we think and why."

When I initially arrived in Singapore, I assumed that the country's educational system was very similar to India's, and I immediately stereotyped it as one that was singularly focused on "memorization." Furthermore, after fifteen years of immersion in (and indoctrination by) American educational institutions, I also assumed that an education system that values memorization must be a bad one. In my interviews with parents and teachers in the Singapore system, however, I encountered a range of views on the degree to which Singapore's system relies on memory work, suggesting that **while it does value memorization, it is also very conceptual, requiring students to think and solve problems**. For example, Sarah, a mother of a third grader in a local Singaporean school, discussed the kinds of questions that her daughter gets on science tests, saying, "No child would be able to answer these questions without a solid conceptual understanding of the material. They require students to think quite a bit about the material they've learned and then apply it in real world situations; for example, they might be asked why certain natural phenomena occur, and would have to draw on their knowledge of scientific concepts to figure out the answer." While one twelve-year-old bemoaned the amount of memorization in the system, another told me that some of her teachers tried to be more creative and move beyond memorization. A student from a different school credited her teachers with offering students a range of creative and conceptual assignments. "The stereotype of Singaporeans only memorizing information is absolutely not true," she asserted.

Certainly, Singapore's education system has been trying to move beyond memorization for many years now, and a close look at their exams and tests reveal that they have begun to move into a more conceptual realm. A recent *Straits Times* article on the 2013 Primary School Leaving Exam (PSLE) described the increasing number of questions that required students to think creatively and critically about material that they had never seen or studied before. Students reported finding the test "more interesting" than other tests they were used to.[28] The Singapore math curriculum, which I think is brilliant, requires students to think conceptually as they frame and solve complex word problems. One student told me about a highly creative project that her chemistry teacher assigned as an alternative to a traditional exam. However, she also mentioned that this project was unusual.

In international tests such as the PISA, Singaporean children not only top the charts for math and science, but they also beat all other countries in the problem-solving category, where they are asked to solve everyday problems such as setting a thermostat or finding the quickest route to a destination. Clearly Singapore is moving beyond memorization in many ways. However, in every conversation I've had with students, parents, and teachers in the local system, they all agree that, despite the changes that are clearly taking place in Singaporean schools, memory work is still very much appreciated even though the amount of content that students

28 Amelia Teng, "Interesting, Tricky PSLE Science Paper Scores Well," *The Straits Times*, October 12, 2013.

need to memorize for their exams is still fairly daunting. **In other words, the focus on higher-order thinking skills in Singapore is not replacing the focus on memorization of core information; both conceptual work and memorization seem to be equally valued**. As Singaporean Minister of Education Heng Swee Keat said, "If creativity is about connecting the dots, you need to have solid dots in the first place or you will have nothing to connect. So a grasp of the basics is necessary."

While Singaporean education has been making a tremendous effort to move beyond an education that centers completely around memory work, the cultural reverence for memorization seems deeply rooted in Asian psyches. Jin Li affirms that the Chinese value memorization greatly; she believes that students really *are* learning. She refers to memorization as "repeated learning," arguing that the process helps Chinese learners gain a "deep impression" of the material. She quotes a student in Hong Kong: "Each time I repeat, I have a new idea of understanding; that is to say I can understand better."[29]

While memorizing information is clearly important, and has proven cognitive benefits, I would argue that it marks the beginning of the learning process, not the end. Problems begin to arise when students and teachers see memorization as an end in itself and don't move beyond it. As a teacher, I see memorization as a first step: make sure that kids have key factual information, and, through "repeated learning," enable them to gain a "deep impression" of the material. But memorization isn't the goal of education. Truly educating students involves not just the dissemination and memorization of information, but also the inculcation of higher-order thinking skills that allow students to consider information critically, to make connections between ideas, and eventually to use information in meaningful ways.

---

29 Jin Li, *Cultural Foundations of Learning*: 138.

EXAM SYSTEMS: Where they take us

Fatima is a petite, pretty Malay-Singaporean mother of two children, a fourteen-year-old son and a ten-year-old daughter. Her children attend local schools in Singapore, where they both study very hard. Fatima told me that she quit her job for a year to help her son study for the PSLE,[30] which all Singaporean students take when they are twelve years old. Make no mistake: the stakes of the PSLE are very, very high. "Check your work carefully. *Every mark counts*," says the message at the end of the test paper; this is no exaggeration. A student's scores on this exam will determine where he attends secondary school, which could determine if and where he goes to college. Fatima is now gearing up for her daughter's PSLE, which is still two years away. However, she is concerned that her daughter may not make it into the Express stream (the accelerated/honors track) as her son did; even with tutoring, her daughter is struggling to achieve the high scores necessary to get into the top streams. Fatima's decision to take a year off work to supervise her children's education is not uncommon in Singapore. Mothers who take a year off–they could be called "tiger mothers," or, as they say in Singapore, "*kiasu* moms"–are part of the culture here. (*Kiasu* is a commonly used word used to describe Singapore's competitive spirit. It is from a Hokkien word that means "afraid to lose.") Those mothers are regarded not with suspicion and judgment, but with sympathy, because they are seen as responsible parents who want to help their children navigate their exam years. This period is highly stressful not only for students but also for their families, particularly mothers, who are often held at least partially responsible for their results.

The Indian and Chinese systems are also highly exam-oriented, with students' fates determined by the scores they get on high-stakes tests. Across Asia, parents lament the stress and anxiety caused

---

30 The PSLE (Primary School Leaving Exam) is a national examination, administered by the Singapore Ministry of Education, that all children in Singapore take at the end of sixth grade in primary school, the results of which will determine the choice of secondary school for each candidate.

by the exams and the brutal competition they engender. Yet they continue unabated, and the pressure seems to increase every year. What's going on? Why, if these exams cause so much stress, do they continue to dominate the lives of children and parents alike?

Jin Li offers an intriguing explanation. She argues that high-stakes exams persist because they are fair and meritocratic, and in relationship-oriented Asia, they are the only way to ensure that college seats and jobs are not automatically allocated only to the relatives, friends, and acquaintances of those in power. In a society that expects its citizens to be loyal to those whom they know, exams are the only way to ensure some degree of fairness. With their right and wrong answers and numerical scores, they represent a standardized, fair measure of a child's knowledge.

Exams also hold faculty and schools responsible and accountable—it is easy to judge a school based on its results. These judgments seem fair and meritocratic. Many Asian mothers I spoke to believe that without exams, teachers across the region wouldn't work as hard. "Exams force the teachers to be accountable," I heard. Without these exams, would students study as hard as they do? Many Asian mothers think not. One told me that it was hard for her to even imagine a system without exams. "How would we know how our kids are performing, and whether they have really mastered all the material, if we didn't have exams? How would we motivate our children to study? Exams are part of school and education."

Finally, exams force teachers to teach to mastery. A student must master a skill to be able to do well on an exam; mere exposure to information and skills is insufficient. In order to gain mastery, students practice the same skills repeatedly in a way that ensures that the skill becomes second nature. Asian exam systems, from Singapore's PSLE to China's Gaokao to Korea and Japan's rigorous university entrance tests, ensure that all students in these countries have solid math and reading skills.

Interestingly, East Asian countries with standardized exam systems tend to benefit students at the bottom of the economic ladder. In his provocative book *Re-Evaluating Education in Japan and*

Korea: Demystifying Stereotypes, Professor Hyunjoon Park of the University of Pennsylvania uses PISA and TIMSS results to show that the bottom students in Japan and Korea[31] perform very well on these tests compared to low performers in other nations. While the top students in America are on par with the top students in Korea and Japan, the bottom students in America are far behind the bottom students in Korea and Japan. Similarly, I am repeatedly amazed that *every child* on the island of Singapore, whether rich or poor, is required to take the extremely rigorous and conceptual PSLE math exam. These exam systems help East Asian nations maintain a high level of baseline education for all citizens: they hold students from disadvantaged backgrounds to the same standards as their more privileged peers, and they force teachers to work hard with all students and ensure that they master the material and skills necessary to pass. In contrast, more individualistic and differentiated systems like those in the US benefit affluent students and shortchange the other kids. While teachers in non-exam systems such as the US are often content to merely *expose* students to information and skills, teachers in competitive and standardized exam systems feel compelled to ensure that all children *master* key skills and content.

This doesn't mean, however, that wealthy Asian kids don't still have a significant advantage over their peers in lower socioeconomic groups. Since wealthy parents can afford the best tutors—the Learning Lab in Singapore costs $60 SGD ($44 USD) per session, for example—their kids obviously have an unfair advantage. **Across Asia, the extensive tutoring system undermines the equalizing nature of a standardized exam system, and top schools and universities have disproportionate numbers of wealthier students**. Even so, the range of PISA scores in East Asian nations remains significantly narrower than in Western countries, revealing that the baseline educational standards in countries like Singapore, Korea, and Japan are very high. In the 2012 PISA, for example, only 8.3

31 Hyunjoon Park, *Re-Evaluating Education in Japan and Korea: Demystifying Stereotypes* (New York: Routledge, 2013).

percent of Singaporean students scored in the lowest bands for mathematics, while 40 percent scored in the top bands. The remaining 51.7 percent presumably scored in the middle bands. This means that the vast majority of students on the island are at least fairly competent at math.

When I first began my teaching career in the US, I spent two years teaching in a very under-resourced, low-performing public school in Baltimore, as part of the Teach For America program. Later on, I volunteered with young children in homeless shelters in Boston. In Singapore, too, I spent a year volunteering at a local community center where I taught reading to low-income children. When I began volunteering in Singapore, I was amazed at the difference between these low-income students and those I worked with in the US. The biggest difference was that they were far better behaved and more respectful than the low-income kids I worked with in the US. In addition, unlike those I encountered in Baltimore and Boston, all the low-income kids I worked with here could pay attention to instructions and follow them appropriately, and at least half of them could read and write somewhat close to their grade levels, if not at grade level.

Despite these observations, I do realize that poverty takes its toll on kids here in Singapore just as it does on kids everywhere in the world. In conversations with educators and academics here who are more familiar with low-income "neighborhood schools," I heard about kids who didn't even show up for their PSLE exams (the teachers had to drive to their house to forcibly pick them up and bring them to school) and students who got into fights in school on a regular basis.

My experiences, while obviously quite limited in their scope, have led me to believe that Singapore (and possibly other high-performing East Asian nations like Korea and Japan) is doing a much better job of educating its low-income students than the US is, perhaps because of the need to educate all children to pass the same rigorous exams. Low-income Singaporean kids, despite their economically disadvantaged backgrounds, do much better than their American counterparts because the national school system is standardized to ensure that all children not only take the same tests but also benefit from equally well-trained and rigorously selected teachers.

Yet exams seem to me to be a double-edged sword. In some ways they remind me of a child's playpen, stocked with good books and educational toys, or a stroller that a modern-day urban mother uses when she takes the child out for walks: these devices keep him safe, encourage him to learn certain things in a controlled environment, and allow the parent to do whatever needs to be done. They're very useful and they keep everything orderly and under control. But they simultaneously restrict the child's level of movement—he can't run through the park or stop to climb a tree when his mother is pushing him along in a stroller. The parent has complete control, and for the most part, the child sees and learns only what the parent wants him to learn. If the child were let loose, who knows what mischief he'd get into. Who knows what he'd choose to explore, and how he'd go about it. Perhaps he'd waste his time, or do something dangerous. On the other hand, perhaps he would do something very inventive, creative, and exciting. Getting rid of the restraints and the limits— letting the child out of the playpen or the stroller—is always risky, but sometimes it's a risk worth taking. Consider the educational alternatives to exams: student-led discussions, projects, presentations, research papers, and internships. While one could argue that the outcomes of these kinds of assignments are far less predictable than exam results, they just might be something spectacular and innovative.

When we give students exams, we're expecting them to give us the right answer to a question. There's nothing wrong with this, but it is a limited way of conceiving the ultimate goal of an education. Sometimes it makes sense for a child, figuratively speaking, to get out of the highly controlled and restrictive stroller and run free, so that she can explore a tree or a park and come up with her own questions. Sometimes, a student learns more by asking the right questions than by figuring out the right answer. Sometimes, a student learns more by generating a range of answers–a whole host of possibilities–as opposed to one "right" answer. Sometimes a student learns more by experimenting and experiencing than by studying a textbook and answering questions. When we hold our students hostage to a high-stakes exam system, we end up eliminating their sense of possibility. We tell them that there is a right answer, they have to learn that answer, and that's that. Where's the room for questioning? For risk-taking? For possibility? For experimentation? For imagination? For independent decisionmaking? For divergent and even disruptive views? Of course, at the risk of making a large generalization, these are precisely the areas where exam-oriented Asian nations are negatively stereotyped and critiqued not only by the West but also by their own citizens. I would argue that many European systems are also quite constrained by national exams. The US is, I think, fairly unique in not having a high-stakes national exam system, and in its willingness to continually experiment with different types of education programs and approaches.

On a tangential note, it's interesting to me that, despite the absence of standardized national exams that determine students' futures, much of the education news in the US revolves around testing and the vast number of tests that students are required to take in public schools. While the new Common Core standards are designed to standardize America's public education system, the Common Core tests are completely different from national exams in Asia and Europe because they have little or no impact on children's individual academic careers. These tests are not used to determine what secondary school or university a child attends, but rather to judge teachers and schools. As a result, while teachers may be very invested in teaching to these tests, students don't invest long hours studying for them, and parents find them more of an annoyance than a purposeful academic goal for their children to work toward. While all the adults in the American system are held accountable for student performances, students themselves are not held accountable for their own performances, even though it is their education and they are the ones taking the tests. The

American approach to testing in public schools is very strange, if you ask me, and it is singularly different from national exam systems in the rest of the world.

Many of the Asian mothers I interviewed are well aware that exam systems have limitations as well as benefits. Fatima, for example, went so far as to say that she would leave Singapore if she could because she feels as though the Singapore educational systems is too stressful for children and parents. She describes herself as a *"kiasu* mom."* When asked why she characterized herself this way, she replied, "Because I feel more anxious about my son's exams than he does." As her daughter gears up for the PSLE, Fatima is increasingly anxious. "My daughter is not strong in math," she said, "and even with regular tuitions [tutoring], she is not doing very well. But since every Singaporean student has to do the PSLE and work within this system, there is no way out."

Having looked long and hard at education systems that both emphasize and de-emphasize memory work, I have decided that when it comes to learning, both traditional educators who revere memory and progressive educators who shun memory in favor of discovery-based learning and conceptual learning are right. Students need to know factual information—not as an end in itself, but as a beginning. They need it so that they can analyze, critique, synthesize and apply what they know, and even more importantly so that they can begin pushing the boundaries of what is known and imagining, discovering, and inventing. Einstein's famous quotation, "Imagination is more important than knowledge," may be true since imagination is unconstrained and infinite, and it can lead us into uncharted terrain in a way that existing knowledge cannot. However, what Einstein forgot to say is that one needs first to know what already exists before he can imagine alternative possibilities. Knowledge is a prerequisite to imagination, but ultimately, both imagination and free, independent thought are very important for both individuals and societies. Our children need discipline to build a strong knowledge base *and* freedom to let their imagination take flight.

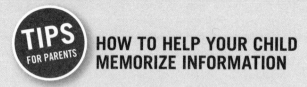

TIPS FOR PARENTS
HOW TO HELP YOUR CHILD MEMORIZE INFORMATION

(These suggestions are adapted from Daniel Willingham's *Why Don't Students Like School?* I highly recommend this book for a far more detailed discussion of memorization and its relationship to cognition.)

- **Encourage your child to consider the meaning of information when she studies**; this will help her remember it. We are much more likely to remember something when we think carefully about what it means. A child who is writing things down without actually focusing on what she's writing won't remember the information. She has to attend to the information and focus on it in order to remember it. We remember things when we actively think about them. (A good example here is the way I often forget where I put my keys or whether I locked the door because I'm thinking about other things while I'm doing these actions. We only remember actions or words if we think about them.)

- **Coming up with good acronyms is a great way to help students remember lists of items**. I often use acronyms to help my students remember bits of information. For example, when I teach students about the use of coordinating conjunctions in grammar (For, And, Nor, But, Or, Yet, So), I use the wonderful (and commonly used) acronym FANBOYS. This really helps students remember the list.

- **Practice, practice, practice, and more practice**: The best way to really internalize information like the multiplication tables or basic math facts is to practice repeatedly on a daily or at least fairly regular basis. Willingham suggests "over-practicing" essential information so it becomes automatic. Once information is so well embcdded in your child's memory that it is automatically recalled without effort or hesitation, then she can focus on higher-order thinking skills. For example, once you know your multiplication tables backwards, you can focus on more complex problems and determine what the problem is asking for and what equation you should use. You won't have to waste time on lower-level mathematical procedures. This frees your mind up to focus on higher-level cognitive tasks.

■ **See that your child spaces out his studying**. Studies show that spacing out studying is better for long-term memory. In other words, if your child reviews material for half an hour every day for a week, he will remember the information for longer than if he studied for four hours the night before the test.

HOW TO ENCOURAGE CRITICAL THINKING SKILLS

You can help your children develop critical thinking skills by asking them open-ended questions about whatever material they are studying or reading. Open-ended questions have more than one right answer. They encourage students to formulate original opinions and generate a range of possibilities. As a parent, you need to be open to your child's answers, even if they are not the same as what you would have given. The idea here is to encourage your child to think for herself and to validate original thoughts. The child needs to feel empowered to offer her own original thoughts and ideas; she has to feel as though her voice and her opinions will be carefully considered and duly valued.

In an ideal world, you would also encourage your child to ask her own open-ended questions. Such questions will ultimately lead to independent and innovative thinking.

Open-ended questions that encourage critical thinking include:

■ What did you think about...? (the book, the recent legislation, etc.) Why do you think that?

■ What else could the character (or politician, or scientist) have done in this situation? Why do you think that?

■ What do you think the author is really saying here? What do his words suggest or reveal?

■ What's your opinion about...? Why? But some people think... Force your child to defend his/her opinion and consider an alternative perspective by playing devil's advocate.

■ What are possible solutions to the problem of...? Explain and defend your solutions.

■ How are these ideas connected to other things you know about?

■ Why are you learning this? Do you think that this is worth learning?

■ Why do you think this information is important? Could it make any difference in the real world? How does this information change how you view the world?

■ Are there things you would like to change about your school? What are they? How could you begin to make that change?

■ Do you agree with this author's (or reporter's, or politician's) view on ...? Why or why not? What would work better?

PART 2

ACHIEVING BALANCE

Making Time for Work and Time for Play and Supporting and Motivating Our Children

Balance is the perfect state of still water. Let that be our model. It remains quiet within and is not disturbed on the surface.

—Confucius (551–479 BC)

Nature does not hurry, yet everything is accomplished.

—Lao Tzu (571–531 BC)

CHAPTER 4

Where Are All The Children?

The sun glints off the surface of the cool water, making the large swimming pool very inviting. But the condo is quiet, and its pool is empty. Where are all the kids, I wonder? It's 5 p.m. on Wednesday evening, but there are no children splashing about in this pool.

The public parks are lush, green, and beautiful. Palm trees sway in the wind, and state-of-the-art playground equipment and comfortable benches wait expectantly for visitors. But it's 5 p.m. on Thursday evening, and no local children are out here playing. Where are all the children?

When I first arrived in Singapore, I was simultaneously impressed and perplexed by the number of sparkling swimming pools and well-manicured public parks and playgrounds in the city. These spaces are beautiful, making this little island feel like a resort, a paradise for children. Nonetheless, these spaces are often empty, particularly during the week; if there are children splashing or running about, they tend to be children who attend international schools—"expat kids." Where are all the local Singaporean children?

There's an easy answer to this question: they are at tuition.

Or they are at home studying.

Or they are in special classes, learning to develop additional talents and skills.

Sample Schedules

I asked many parents about their children's schedules. Here are some samples:

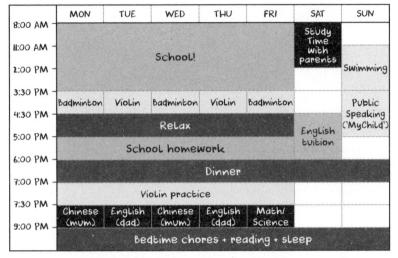

Sam, Chinese student in a local primary school in Singapore, age nine

Rohan, Indian student at an international school, age nine

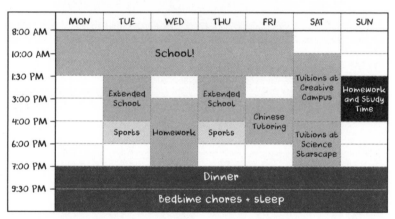

	MON	TUE	WED	THU	FRI	SAT	SUN
8:00 AM	School!					Study Time with parents	
12:00 PM							
	Lunch + Additional mandarin program at school						
3:00 PM	Snack + Relax!					Study Time with parents	
4:00 PM							
	Learning Lab	Swimming	Learning Lab	Gym			
6:00 PM							
	School homework + Learning Lab						
7:30 PM	Dinner						
8:30 PM							
	Story + Bedtime						

Amelia, Chinese-Singaporean Student at a local kindergarten, age six

	MON	TUE	WED	THU	FRI	SAT	SUN
8:00 AM	School!						
10:00 AM							
1:30 PM						Tuitions at Creative Campus	Homework and Study Time
3:00 PM		Extended School		Extended School			
4:00 PM					Chinese Tutoring		
		Sports	Homework	Sports		Tuitions at Science Starscape	
6:00 PM							
7:00 PM	Dinner						
9:30 PM							
	Bedtime chores + sleep						

Cayden, Chinese-Singaporean student in a local school in Singapore, age twelve

NIGHT-OWL SCHEDULES

Fatima, the outgoing and chatty mother we met in chapter 3, is an administrative assistant at a school. Her son Ahmed did well on his PSLE (Primary School Leaving Exam, the high-stakes national exam that Singaporean children take in sixth grade), for which she took a year off from work, and he is now in eighth grade at a good local secondary school. Having returned to work, she has a busy schedule each day, arriving at the office by 8 a.m. and leaving around 5 p.m.

She often runs errands on her way home, as she picks up groceries or food for dinner. Yet, after a full day of work, she still spends many hours at night helping her children with their schoolwork.

Fourteen-year-old Ahmed does not attend extra enrichment classes outside of school. His extracurricular activities involve only the mandatory co-curricular activities that the school offers, which he does twice a week. When he comes home from school, he has a snack and then takes a three-hour nap from 4 to 7 p.m. He wakes up in time for evening prayers with his family, who are Muslim, and then begins to study. Twice a week, a tutor comes to the house to work with him from 7:30 to 9 p.m. Fatima bemoaned the costs of these tuitions, which eat into her monthly salary considerably. "But what to do? Without tuitions, it's very hard to do well," she said. After tuition, Ahmed finishes up his homework, usually by 10 p.m., and then unwinds with television and family time for an hour or two before going to sleep. On days when he doesn't have tuition, he spends his time studying and doing homework from 7:30 to 10 p.m. or so, and then enjoys an hour or two of TV. Either way, he normally goes to sleep well after 11 p.m, often after midnight.

In a number of conversations, I heard about similar schedules; apparently it is quite common for students to take naps right after school and then stay up late to study. One local math teacher who tutors in the evenings told me that most of her tutoring sessions are held between 7 and 9 p.m.; her latest tutoring session ends at 10 p.m. Similarly, many of the music schools in my neighborhood offer piano and violin classes for young kids late into the evening; one first-grader I know has a piano class from 7:30 to 8:30 p.m. on Friday evening. Clearly, these night-owl schedules are far from unusual in Singapore. On a practical note, they allow working parents like Fatima to spend time with their children and supervise their studying closely, but they may also result in exhausted, overextended children.

Research suggests that chronic sleep deprivation and exhaustion are a leading cause not just of physical ailments and low immunity but also of mental illnesses like depression. As a high-school teacher at top private schools in the US and in Singapore, I have often been startled when my students walk into class dragging their feet and then proceed to slump into their chairs, their eyes sleepy and their faces careworn. When I ask them if they're okay, they regale me with stories of early-morning sports practice, evening drama rehearsals, and late nights spent studying. In Singapore, though, it's not just teens who are exhausted; kids of all ages seem to be getting less sleep than they need. A 10 p.m. bedtime for elementary school kids is not unusual here.

THE TUITION TREADMILL

While the playgrounds in Singapore may be empty during the week, the tuition centers are always full. Tuition centers are a booming business here in Singapore and all across Asia. Parents spend a very high proportion of their income on these services, and the time and money invested in the tuition industry is staggering. East Asian and South Asian kids who attend international schools often have extra math classes to supplement a Western math education that is perceived as lacking in rigor, as well as extra enrichment classes of all kinds. The Indian mothers I talked to were trying to do it all—math coaching, science and robotics classes, music, art, and a sport. Many of my East Asian students described their packed after-school schedules to me—language classes in their mother tongue, along with extra math and English classes. And this is not a phenomenon unique to Asian parents wanting to enhance their children's international school education; children in the local school system are also often burdened by lots of extra "tuition" classes.

In a recent *Straits Times* article, senior education correspondent Sandra Davie reported some startling numbers based on studies done by the National Institute of Education in Singapore. Between 1998 and 2008, tuition spending in Singapore nearly doubled, from $410 million to $800 million SGD ($300–$600 million USD).[32]

---

32 Sandra Davie, "NIE Studying Impact of Tuition," *The Straits Times* (September 28, 2013).

These numbers are mindboggling, considering that Singapore has a total population of just over 5 million, of which only approximately 1 million are of the tuition-going ages of three to eighteen.

While these numbers seem incredible, I believe them. All the parents I interviewed for this book send their kids for some kind of tuition. Lei, a mother of two girls—Amelia, age six, and Corliss, age four—spends $8,000 SGD (nearly $6,000 USD) a year on math and English classes at an expensive tuition center in Singapore. She told me that there is a long waiting list to get into the competitive center her daughters attend, and students have to take an assessment test before they are accepted. Lei believes that the money is worth it, though. She says the new methods used by schools in Singapore are confusing to her (she didn't grow up with model drawing for math, for example), so she'd rather have a trained teacher help her daughters. Furthermore, her friends and cousins have all assured her that children need tuition to ace their exams. "The school teaches 70 percent of what's on the exam, and the tuition centers teach the remaining 30 percent," she said. She went on to explain that teachers now stress independent learning more than they used to, and they don't have enough time to really make kids practice and master key skills, so students have to rely on tuition centers to fill the gaps.

Singapore's obsession with tuition is not unique in Asia. A 2012 article[33] in *Time* magazine by Alice Park reported that nine out of ten South Korean elementary pupils have private tutoring, as do six out of ten primary school students in India's West Bengal. In Hong Kong, 85 percent of senior secondary students receive tutoring, and companies advertise the services of "star" tutors on television, newspapers, and the backs of buses.

The amount of money spent by Koreans and Japanese on supplementary education is astounding. Park reports that Japan spent $12 billion on private tutoring in 2010. The *New York Times* has

33 AFP article, "Asian Spending Billions on Tutors," July 5, 2012. http://
sg.news.yahoo.com/asia-spending-billions-tutors-study-223633801.html.

run stories on star tutors in Korea who make over a million dollars a year.

All the Asian mothers I interviewed in Singapore, whether they send their children to local or international schools, engage at least one private tutor or send their children to a tutoring center—usually for math or Chinese, but often also for English and science. I think it is very rare for a middle- or upper-class Asian child over the age of five *not* to attend some sort of tuition center in Singapore, regardless of whether she is enrolled in a local school or an international school. From my limited sampling, I think that students in the local school system tend to have more tuition, and certainly more academic pressure, than their peers in the international systems. In fact, one mother estimated that thirty out of the thirty-five students in her son's class at the Anglo-Chinese School attended tuitions *in all their major academic subjects*. Her son himself spends all day Saturday at tuition classes.

Similarly, Pooja, whose daughter had just finished the dreaded PSLE, told me that she had spent close to $20,000 SGD ($15,000 USD) on tuitions for her daughter in the year leading up to the PSLE. She seemed worn out by both the stress and the expense associated with the high-stakes test administered to twelve-year-olds.

ASIAN PARENTS SPEAK OUT

"My daughter doesn't need tuition"

"I know I'm swimming against the tide. And I don't know how long I'll be able to do it. But for now, I'm not convinced that tuitions are the best thing for my girls. I do, however, spend a lot of time working with them on their homework and helping them with their studies. I buy them workbooks so that they can practice their skills independently. Last year, for example, Sophia was struggling with math. She found it hard to solve word problems, and I realized that she was confused about the logic behind them. So I sat down with her and we worked through some of the problems together. That really helped her. And for as long as I can help her, she doesn't need tuitions."

—**Faith Lee**, mother of Sophia (eight) and Lily (six)

Her daughter, too, seemed exhausted. When I asked her daughter what she had learned from the PSLE, she told me, "I learned how to deal with lots of stress. Unlike many of my friends, I can still laugh and smile even when exams are going on." Asia's tuition frenzy is legendary; phrases like "educational pressure cooker," "education fever," "exam obsession," and "paper-qualification society" abound, reflecting the intense emphasis that these societies place on formal education.

The tuition treadmill is not restricted to upper-class students on the island. Many parents from lower income levels spend a substantial amount of money on tuitions. This is also true of neighboring China and India. The quality of tuitions and tutors varies based on cost, but the fact remains that across the board, parents in Asia rely heavily on tutors and tuition centers.

Clearly, parents across Asia would not send their children to tuition centers and "shadow schools" (private tuition centers that kids attend to review what they learned at school) if they believed these extra hours of individualized attention were unnecessary. While there are many drawbacks to tuition (such as the amount of time it takes up that could be devoted to free play and time in nature), there are also some real advantages to individualized tutorials, particularly for students who need to master crucial skills for high-stakes exams.

DO STUDENTS REALLY NEED TUITION? Confronting the limitations of classroom teachers and the benefits of individualized instruction

Imagine this scene, which could take place in a twenty-first-century school anywhere in the world:

An earnest and energetic teacher stands in front of a class of thirty kids and introduces a new science concept to her students. She has made an effort to make the concept come alive for the class: she is using colorful images on a projector to help illustrate her point, and she tries to use interesting analogies and humor to not only help her students understand the concept but also keep them engaged. Of the thirty students, ten have very solid backgrounds in science, so the concept makes total sense to them. They are listening closely, taking notes, and nodding their heads. Another ten students see what the teacher is talking about, but the concept is fuzzy and shadowy in their minds. They listen, laughing at the jokes and gazing at the images, but not really understanding her words very well. Of the remaining ten students, two are half asleep, with their mouths slightly open. Three are secretly checking Facebook on their smartphones, smiling at all the new status updates. Two are surreptitiously passing notes to each other at the back. Three are daydreaming and doodling in their notebooks, wondering about lunch or panicking about the math test they will soon have to take.

The teacher, who is genuinely invested in making sure her students learn, goes on to engage the kids in a group activity to help them get a hands-on understanding of the concept she just explained. She puts students into mixed-ability groups and gives them an interesting experiment to carry out. In theory, mixed-ability group work is an opportunity for weaker students to develop their skills by working alongside stronger students to complete a task. But as often happens, the strongest kids in each group take the lead and do all the work. The mid-range kids, those who see, but through a fog, watch and try to be helpful, furthering their hazy understanding of what's going on. And the daydreamers and sleepers continue to daydream, sleep, or chat with each other.

At the end of the lesson, the teacher asks some concept-checking questions to see if her lesson has been understood. Many—but not all—hands go up, and several students provide the answers she is looking for. The teacher leaves feeling satisfied that she has done her very best to teach a complex scientific concept. The students leave with varying degrees of understanding: a third get it, a third have a vague understanding of the concept, and a third have absolutely no idea what's going on.

While it's easy to blame teachers when students don't pick up crucial skills, they rarely acknowledge the limitations of a large classroom. The fact of the matter is that students often need individualized attention, not only to help them focus, but also to help them understand and master a concept or skill.

WESTERN TRENDS IN EDUCATION: Moving toward individualized instruction

Over the last few years, Western teachers have been repeatedly told that their role in the classroom is changing. They are no longer supposed to be the "sage on the stage," they are now expected to be the "guide on the side." Most books on twenty-first-century skills, from Ian Gilbert's *Why Do I Need A Teacher when I've Got Google?* to Sal Khan's bestseller *The One World Schoolhouse*, urge teachers to be "mentors," "guides," and "facilitators" who help students work on projects of their own choosing at their own pace. Contemporary educational wisdom suggests that given the wide access that students have to information through the internet, they don't need live teachers to "teach" them; what students need instead are inspiring adults who will give them *individual attention* while they work on projects that they find exciting and motivating.

I find this new approach to education appealing on some levels and somewhat frustrating on others. While I have my doubts about many aspects of such educational fads and trends, there is one aspect of this new approach to learning that does ring true: **children do benefit from individualized attention that helps them with what they need at the pace that's best for them**.

Over the last few years, I have experimented with individualized instruction in my classroom in a number of ways. I spend a lot of time on "reading conferences" and "writing conferences,"–conversations between a teacher and a student about her reading or writing–and as a result, I'm a strong believer in the power of individualized instruction. One-on-one instruction helps students for the following reasons:

- When I sit down individually with a student, **I can instruct and guide a student at his own level**. If he is struggling with subject-verb agreement, I can explain this concept to him. If my student is confused about the author's portrayal of a particular character, I can discuss the character with him in more detail and point him to key passages that he needs to look at. I can ask him specific questions to help him refine his thinking. In an individualized session, **the student sets the pace and the agenda: we work on what he needs in a way that is beneficial to him**.

- The student is far less self-conscious about asking questions because he doesn't have to worry about his peers' judgments. He can ask questions that he wouldn't ask in a whole-class setting.
- As a teacher, I can give a student immediate feedback during an individualized conference. She can write out a sample analysis or sentence for me, and I can critique it on the spot in an individualized conference.
- There is no option for a student to daydream, zone out, chat with friends, or check Facebook because my attention as a teacher is completely focused on her. In contrast, in a whole-class setting, many students don't actually pay attention to what the teacher is saying. (Surprise, surprise!)
- Individualized sessions cement the teacher-student relationship. The student knows the teacher is actively concerned about his academic performance. This relationship is a source of motivation for student and teacher alike.

What I'm really doing when I work individually with students is giving them *individualized tutorials*. In fact, in Asia, we might call these reading and writing conferences a form of tuition. Unfortunately, in most classrooms, the number of students precludes this kind of individualized tutorial. Even at the private school where I work, the numbers make this kind of conferencing a challenge. I tend to have around twenty students in a class. When I tell my students that they have time to work on their essays or presentations or projects while I conference with each of them individually, I know that some of my students will waste their time in one way or another. Since they all have their own laptops, some of them will pretend to work while they surf the web, update their Facebook status, or chat with each other online. So while each student gains a lot from the ten-minute conference with me, they also end up having more than an hour of time to work independently, which they may or may not use well. In other words, the opportunity cost of individualized instruction may also be quite high in a classroom setting. **Individualized instruction works much better in the home setting, in small group sessions as at Asian-style tuition centers or shadow schools, or in individualized tutoring sessions**.

An average classroom in Singapore has forty students. A classroom in a top-tier elite Indian school may have well over thirty-five students, and second-tier Indian schools may have more than fifty students per class. In China, classes in lower secondary school often have close to fifty students, and top-ranked Gaokao schools often have up to sixty children in a class. Given these class sizes, it is virtually impossible for a teacher to have individual conferencing with students. No wonder students turn to private, individualized tuition: that is often the only way for them to gain the one-on-one targeted instruction and scaffolding that they need to progress academically.

The growing obsession, both in Asia and the West, with phenomena such as shadow schooling, private tuition, and home schooling are all in one way or another an acknowledgement that students often learn more, learn faster, and learn better when they receive *individualized* instruction. The booming tuition industry is also evidence that middle- and upper-class parents will do everything they can to give their children an advantage over their peers. In an increasingly competitive world where everyone sees education as the key to upward mobility and opportunity, parents often feel private tuitions are the only way to help their children keep up and get ahead. There is also something insidiously competitive about the tuition phenomenon. If, as a parent, you know that every other kid is getting tutored, you feel intense pressure to keep your child "on par" by enrolling him in extra classes. When tutoring is the norm, it is hard to buck the trend.

WHY DO SCHOOLS AND GOVERNMENTS DISLIKE TUITIONS?

While parents and students across Asia tend to swear by tutors and tuitions, official institutions such as schools and governments tend to abhor them. They worry that tuition becomes a crutch, preventing students from tackling challenging academic work independently. As one math teacher told me, "The tragedy of children who are coached and tutored is that they don't have the thrill of discovering the right method and answer themselves. Tutoring is like spoon-feeding a child." There is certainly some truth to this viewpoint.

At a macro level, governments and policymakers worry that tuitions will increase educational inequalities; children from affluent families will become more successful because of private tutoring, while children from low-income families will fall further behind. Most education experts see tuition as unnecessary at best and dangerous at worst.

What I find interesting about such reactions, however, is that they fail to acknowledge the role that school administrators and policy makers play in fuelling the tuition industry. Don't they see the limitations of large classrooms? Don't they recognize the finite time and energy that classroom teachers have? And don't they notice how tracking and high-stakes national exams create the competition that pushes parents towards tuition centers?

A classroom teacher in high school who teaches well over a hundred students every day can't possibly spend twenty or even ten minutes individually with each student. For bright and self-motivated students who can teach themselves using resources such as textbooks, websites, or videos, individualized instruction may be unnecessary. A highly competent and motivated student is probably better off figuring things out for herself. Contemporary Western educational rhetoric seems aimed at these top students who are motivated enough and bright enough to learn independently from online and print resources.

For an average or struggling student, however, getting individualized attention may make the difference between failure and success. In an ideal world, the classroom teacher and the parent would be the adults who provide children with targeted individualized instruction and immediate feedback. However, since it's not viable for teachers to do this, given the number of children per class, the responsibility ends up on the parents' shoulders. While many parents do tutor their own children by supervising homework, supplementing it with extra resources, and offering students explicit instructional support, there are times when they find they don't have the time or the knowledge and skills necessary to provide this sort of individualized instruction. Or parents get frustrated with their children, and they dislike the battles and tensions that arise over homework and studying. At this point, they tend to turn to tutors.

So while educators and experts may denigrate the idea of tuitions and condemn parents who fuel the trend by hiring tutors, parents and children often find tremendous security and comfort in the help that a tutor is able to give.

WHAT ASIAN MOTHERS SAY ABOUT PLAY

Listening to parents tell me about their children's busy schedules made me wonder whether Asian kids on the island ever have time to play. Childhood and play have been synonymous through history. "Go play," we tell our kids, because play is what children do naturally. So one warm evening, I met with a group of Indian mothers at a playground to ask them about their views toward *free play; that is,* play that is not structured and driven by adults. We mothers sat on benches, watching our children chase each other up and down the slide. Observing the delight and excitement on the kids' faces as they ran around, I couldn't help smiling. There are few sights more soothing than that of children playing. When I lived in New York City, I routinely encountered parents and early-childhood educators who romanticized play—"play is the work of childhood," they would say—and I can understand why. When else can we be magical superheroes with powers that allow us to save the world from invading aliens? And when else can we view the world from the branches of a wide tree or the very top of the jungle-gym, full of awe at our own strength and skill? When else but in childhood can we blow and chase bubbles, laughing with glee at their ephemeral beauty? When else can we glide down a slide for the pure joy of movement? Through play, children express their imagination, exuberance, and wonder, and what work could possibly be more important than that for our kids?

Anita from Kolkata agreed with me. "I want my children to go down to the playground in the evenings and play because I remember playing like that when I was a child. All the children in my apartment building would come down to play in the evenings. The boys would play cricket, the girls would play badminton, and we would chat and hang out together. But where's the time? Between activities and academics, our children's schedules are just so jam-packed these days. You don't want to be the only mother who is not making your child play a sport and learn an instrument. And if children don't do supplementary math like Kumon or Abacus, then they fall behind in math. So given how competitive and fast-paced things are these days, where's the time for that kind of old-fashioned play?"

Meera agreed. "I wonder what the end result of all these activities and tuitions will be? Will it all matter or not?" She added, "I do let my children play in the evenings because it's healthy for them."

However, Jhanvi, mother of ten-year-old Malvika, disagreed. "Our children do so many extracurricular activities that we never had access to when we were young. They are so privileged and lucky to be able to do art and gymnastics and piano. These kids have everything. We are investing everything in them, so they need to work hard and do well."

There was a chorus of agreement:

"It's true. Our children today have so many more opportunities than we had one generation ago–"

"When you are given so much, you also need to do well!"

"Our children know that we have all our hopes and

aspirations invested in them. They know how much we sacrifice to give them all these opportunities."

In my interviews with other Singaporean parents, I heard a similar range of views on "play." When I asked Fatima whether her son Ahmed had free time to go out and play, she responded, "Play, play, play is all very good, but it won't get my son good results. I encourage him to go out with his friends for a few hours on the weekend. He is a good boy, and it's important for him to go out and have some fun with his friends. They go to East Coast Park on Sunday afternoons, and they'll often go skateboarding. But beyond that, there's really no time for play. The competition these days is intense, and he has to do well. He knows it's important, too. Even when I tell him to go play, often he will say that he needs to study."

Li Yan, a Chinese-Singaporean mother, looked surprised by the question. She shook her head and answered, "These days, if you let children play, they turn on a television or a video game. I think it's better for them to do organized activities than just play on a gadget. These gadgets are no good. Look at my nephew. He can't stop playing video games. My children are not allowed to watch television or play video games during the week. They can play for two hours on the weekend, but that's it."

With my own children, I often struggle to find that perfect balance between work and play, and I've often wrestled with the following questions:

- How much supplementary academic work is healthy? How do I make sure my children are not only gaining all the foundational academic skills they need, but also finding enough time to play, read, and daydream?
- How do I cope with my own anxieties as a parent? When other people's children are doing hours of extra tuitions and extra enrichment classes, how do I stick to my own philosophy of balance?
- In a world that is increasingly fast-paced, action-packed and task-oriented, how do I make sure that my children and I find

time and space for quiet contemplation and solitude? (This is probably as much an issue for adults as it is for children—I often crave time to just read and think, but feel instead that I lurch from one task to the next so that I can cross out all the items on my ever-expanding to-do list.)

I consider these questions on a regular basis, and I never feel quite satisfied that I'm getting the balance right with my own two children. I make sure that they go out to play from 5:30 to about 6:45 every evening, and I would like to make sure that they continue to get this unstructured, outdoor playtime for as long as possible. While these hours seem very late by American standards, they are perfectly normal in Singapore. Kids here don't go out to play until 5:30 or 6 p.m., partly because it's too hot before that and partly because they have to finish their classes and studies before their mothers will let them out. However, because I have held this daily unstructured outdoor time sacred, I struggle to fit in everything else that I'd like to do with my kids: supplementary math lessons once or twice a week (I'm an Asian mom living in Singapore; how can I not make my kids do a little extra math each week?), a short supplementary grammar lesson once a week (I'm an English teacher, after all, and formal grammar is increasingly de-emphasized in progressive schools), some time devoted to the arts and sports, lots of free reading and read-alouds...and then there's school homework. And I want my kids in bed by 8 or 8:30 p.m. at the very latest. It feels like an impossible challenge to fit it all in! I find myself constantly adjusting my kids' schedules as I try to find that perfect (but elusive) balance between structured learning and unstructured play.

My son is now nine, and I've found that I'm doing less active academic supplementing at home with him than I used to. He now has afterschool activities at school as well as a substantial homework load, so whatever supplementary work I do with him is relegated to a few hours on the weekend. I believe that it's very important for him to complete his school homework independently, so during the week, that is is what he does. In contrast, I spend more time actively supplementing my daughter's learning at home, since, at age six, she has fewer demands from school. For working mothers like me, supplementing during the work week is a real challenge—I come home from my job exhausted, and I often don't have the time or energy to work with my kids as much as I would like to.

I am impressed by the dedication of other Asian mothers to their children's academic lives. Even when they outsource much of the academic supplementing to outside tutors, they still manage to do an awful lot of coaching and supervision to ensure their kids are completing homework assignments, working hard, and learning all they need to. Some working mothers even speak with their bosses about altering their schedules so that they can go home early at least one afternoon a week to offer their kids homework help.

Most of the mothers I spoke with—working moms as well as stay-at-home moms—agreed that they had the most leeway to both "teach" their children core skills and content as well as choose

ASIAN PARENTS SPEAK OUT

"I schedule time for play"

"My daughters' schedules sound pretty typical at first: they have school from 7:20 a.m. to 1:30 p.m., followed by the usual round of extracurricular activities (ballet, swimming, and Chinese enrichment classes). But other Singapore moms are always shocked when I tell them that I also schedule time for play—every day, from 5:30 to 7 p.m., they play with their friends in the playground or gardens. I believe play is very important, and I am quite sure that when my girls look back on their childhoods, they will thank me for letting them play every day. They learn so much from playing outside with their friends—conflict resolution, how to share, how to interact with children from different backgrounds. I can't possibly teach those lessons at home. Many other Singaporean mothers only want to invest time and money in activities that produce instant and easily quantifiable learning. They don't realize that giving children time to play will produce results in the long run. It will take a generation to see these results, though."

—**Faith Lee**, mother of Sophia (eight) and Lily (six)

enrichment activities for their kids in the early years. Parents tend to do a lot with their kids from birth to age eight or nine, but by about third grade, the school seems to dictate what kids learn and do. Since research consistently indicates that a child's educational outcomes can be predicted fairly accurately based on his reading skills and study habits in third grade, perhaps parents are wise to supplement more actively in the early years. If parents ensure that their kids have strong reading, writing, and math skills along with good study habits and attention spans, by third grade, then the kids should be primed to do well in middle and high school.

FINDING A BALANCE: The importance of nature

When discussing tuition-laden schedules and lack of play time for Asian students, with parents, one of the most thought-provoking responses I got came from Li Jie, a Chinese teacher from Wuhan who has a son in the eighth grade of an international school. Soft-spoken and calm, she said that she draws on the philosophies of Buddhism and Taoism, which advocate balance—what the Chinese call *ping heng*. She said, "As a parent, I want my son to relax. He has very high standards for himself, and I feel that I need to help him control his stress. I encourage him to do things that he finds pleasurable and fun, and I encourage him to follow his interests because we all need balance, or *ping heng*, in our lives. Having grown up in China until he turned twelve, my son has imbibed the Chinese values of discipline and hard work. Sometimes I tell him to stop studying and go to sleep, but he says that he cannot fall asleep with the knowledge that he has not tried as hard as he could. I have to help him find that balance—to know when to stop, when to rest, when to relax and take a walk in nature. Our Buddhist philosophers have always advocated balance, a middle path, and they have always said that we can find peace and healing in Mother Nature. I need to remind my son of these age-old Asian lessons."

It is true that across Asia, philosophers, monks, and sages have sought answers to life's questions in the forests and mountains. I have always found Chinese poetry and art calming and beautiful, because these works draw on the richness of nature to reflect the beauty and pathos of human existence. In Indian myths, too, the forest is seen as the natural place to search for wisdom. At the end of each person's life, the final stage involves renouncing society and returning to nature. Perhaps, as Li Jie says, we can all draw comfort and inspiration from older Asian literature and philosophy.

I believe that if play is the work of childhood, then nature is where that work gets done best. Instead of constantly rushing our children along congested highways from one concrete structure to the next, perhaps we need to take some time to return our children to a natural environment: green spaces without the clutter, congestion, and madness of our twenty-first-century urban lives.

Imagine a child staring at a snail, wondering what it would be like to travel with a house on his back. And then taking a small twig and gently poking the snail's soft body and watching it disappear, quick as light, into its little shell house. Then, taking a step back, the child looks up, up, up at the treetops and the blue sky. We are so small—so like the snail—in a large, mysterious world. Imagine the child's sense of wonder and awe as he explores this vast world and begin to consider his place in it.

But if our kids barely have time to play, then how can they possibly have time to experience nature's beauty and develop a sense of wonder? Have you ever gone outside for a walk when you're feeling exhausted and stressed? What happens? Chances are that if you take a walk in a green place with trees, flowers, and birds, you will immediately feel your body and mind relax. So often, after hours of reading and working indoors, I've found my back muscles knotted and tense, my head aching. Often, when I feel like this, I take a walk in the public gardens not far from my apartment. Green spaces and bougainvillea are very therapeutic. As I walk by the river, hot sun on my back and green trees all around, the knots in my back muscles relax a bit, and the throbbing in my head subsides. There are many studies that show how nature can calm and heal people; it can relieve anxiety and is a natural antidote to depression.

In fact, in his book *Biophilia,* renowned scientist Edward O. Wilson examines the innate need that we humans have to connect with nature, for our own physical and emotional well-being. Nature is a tremendous de-stressor and healer, and all people—children, teens and adults—benefit from an hour a day in nature's healing arms. I call this a "green hour," a term I got from Richard Louv's wonderful book on the relationship between children and nature, *Last Child in the Woods.*

Poets and writers have always understood the power of nature to heal us, still our troubled thoughts, humble us, and make us happy. In Willa Cather's novel *My Antonia*, the narrator describes the happiness he finds in nature: "The earth was warm under me, and warm as I crumbled it through my fingers...I kept as still as I could...I was something that lay under the sun and felt it, like the pumpkins, and I did not want to be anything more. I was entirely happy...that is happiness; to be dissolved into something complete and great."[34]

In almost all my interviews, "What about outdoor play?" was a question I often asked. Susan Chan, whose twelve-year-old son's busy schedule includes tuition from 9 a.m to 4 p.m on Saturdays, gave the following response. "Well, Cayden's father and I take him out a lot during the school holidays. That's when we have the time to go cycling or go to the beach. During the school term, there's just too much else to do and too much pressure. He spends all of Saturday at tuitions, and Sunday is for homework, revision, and a family meal." Another mother, Lei, shook her head and said, "Singapore is much too hot. We don't really like the heat and sun, so we prefer to keep Amelia and Corliss indoors. They have swimming lessons every week, and they go to a park or beach once every month or two, but we do take them to indoor play areas sometimes on a Sunday afternoon."

Cayden, Amelia, and Corliss are not alone. Childhood in Singapore has clearly moved indoors: to classrooms, tuition centers,

34 Willa Cather, *My Antonia* (Boston: Houghton Mifflin, 1918): 14

and homes. Singapore has one of the world's highest incidences of myopia, and children here suffer from myriad eye problems. A 2012 article in *Time* magazine quotes a study from the journal *Lancet* stating that up to 90 percent of young adults in major East Asian countries are myopic, compared to only 20 to 30 percent in Western countries. In Singapore, the high rates of nearsightedness in all three major ethnic groups—Chinese, Malays, and Indians—have steadily increased since 1996.[35] One explanation for this is that children are not spending enough time outdoors where they have to look at objects that are far away from them, and where they can see horizons and vistas. When children spend all their time indoors hunched over books and laptops, their eyes become trained to look at objects that are close by, and their long-distance vision suffers greatly. In addition to eye problems, children today often seem exhausted because they are spending so much time indoors. Nature and fresh air invigorate and energize kids, while too much time studying depletes them. In *Last Child in the Woods*, Louv asserts, "Time in nature is not leisure time; it's an essential investment in our children's health."[36]

Nature is not only a boon to physical health; it is also a wonderful antidote to the anxiety that Asian children and their parents have to deal with when confronted with high-stakes exams. Nature provides our children with free therapy: green spaces and exercise make their eyes sparkle, their legs begin to run, their bodies relax. While structured activities in natural settings (sports, for example, or a nature walk supervised by an adult) can be very healthy, Louv suggests that *unstructured* time in nature is perhaps the most valuable for young children. Arguing that the space, freedom, and beauty of nature allow our minds to think freely, he provides studies and anecdotes that document the ways in which time in nature is

35 Alice Park, "Why Up to 90% of Asian Schoolchildren are Nearsighted," *Time*, May 7, 2012, http://healthland.time.com/2012/05/07/why-up-to-90-of-asian-schoolchildren-are-nearsighted.

36 Richard Louv, *Last Child in the Woods* (Chapel Hill, NC: Algonquin Books, 2008): 120.

beneficial. For example, children who play in natural, green spaces tend to play far more creatively than those who play in artificially constructed playgrounds.

Freedom—both physical and mental—is also a prerequisite for creativity. Our children need time when they're allowed to play freely indoors and outdoors, without adults constantly telling them what to do, so they can begin to nurture the creativity that flowers so naturally in them. While Louv's research looks almost exclusively at American families, whom he claims suffer from a "nature-deficit disorder," his conclusions about the need for children to spend time in nature are universal. Parents may think that the opportunity cost of spending time in nature is high (kids could be studying a little bit more instead of "wasting time" playing), but the opposite is actually true. The opportunity cost of not spending time in nature is very high—a huge body of research suggests that our bodies and minds need the natural world, and our children need time outdoors every day to stay physically, mentally, and emotionally healthy.

THE BENEFITS OF UNSTRUCTURED TIME

With all the activities and studying that our children do, where's the time to imagine, play, take risks, run free, and dream? Where's the time for all those activities that don't provide immediate tangible results but *do* lead children to become creative and self-motivated adults? If a child is always told what to do, how will she be able to come up with her own ideas for how to do things? If a child has no time to dream, how will she imagine and create something beautiful and new? If a child has no time to explore her own interests—reading a book for fun, drawing a picture, writing a poem, imagining a story, making a car out of Legos, designing a house of blocks—how will she develop and nurture her passions?

Einstein apparently spent a large chunk of his childhood imagining what it would feel like to ride on a beam of light. These wild imaginings may seem futile and unproductive to a pressured, anxious parent, but they are often the seeds of creativity and innovation. Parents must have faith in these intangible and seemingly wasteful activities–daydreaming and playing are valuable pastimes that will yield sweet and interesting fruit in the future.

Two years ago, I took my son to a birthday party where I met Lisa, a Singaporean-Chinese mother. Lisa and I got along really well; we had many common interests and experiences. We had both spent time studying and working in America, and we were both very interested in Asian parenting issues. As we talked about our children, I happened to ask her why so few Singaporean children play outside in the pools and playgrounds that cover the island. She responded, "We Singaporeans tend to trust tangible things like books, worksheets, exams, and results. We like what is orderly, systematic, and predictable. We get nervous about all those intangibles because they are hard to teach and measure, and the results are often unpredictable and a little messy. But what many Singaporean don't realize is that those intangible qualities– confidence, self-esteem, creativity, imagination, the ability to take risks, interpersonal skills, empathy–are often more crucial to success than all the tangibles put together. As a culture, we need to have faith that our children will benefit from activities that don't yield an immediate tangible result. We need to have faith that an hour spent playing in nature or painting for fun is worthwhile." I couldn't agree more. Many of our children's most valuable learning experiences don't come with a tangible outcome and a numerical score.

But, in Singapore and across Asia, parents and educators are somewhat obsessed with tangible outcomes and numerical scores. It's an exam culture, and those scores matter–they matter tremendously. So parents are always walking a tightrope, caught in a real dilemma: how do they navigate and survive the education fever that grips Asian societies in a calm and balanced way? How can they ensure that their children do well in school, but also have the time and space to play?

My own feelings about "tuitions" and "enrichment" activities are somewhat mixed. As an educator, I can see clear value in one-on-one help for a child who is either struggling or gifted. I believe much of the success that Asian students experience academically can be attributed to all the supplementary educators—parents, tutors, enrichment teachers—who work with them on a daily basis. Growing up in India, I had my fair share of "tuitions," particularly for math and Hindi, and I don't think that I would have done as well in all my exams without those extra classes.

Despite the value I can see in tuitions, they are also a slippery slope. Tuition in one or two subjects may be very helpful, but when I hear of students like Cayden and his classmates, who have tuition in *all* their major subjects, I begin to wonder about the high costs of this system—and I'm not just talking about money. When I talk to my Korean students who tell me about the long hours at the cram schools known as *hagwons* in Korea, I begin to think that many Asian families are overvaluing academic work at the expense of all the other aspects of learning and childhood. So, all things considered, I believe that tuitions can be very helpful for subjects where a child really needs help or subjects where his school just isn't delivering adequately. Beyond that, children should work through their homework on their own, and they should certainly have sufficient unstructured time to pursue activities of their own choice.

No matter how important those test scores may seem, I feel strongly that academic success should never come at the cost of a child's physical and emotional health. We parents have to have faith in the value of play and nature, in the value of all those intangible learning experiences that will help our children develop confidence, creativity, imagination, and empathy. As we plan how to supplement our children's lives, we should remember that Asian philosophies—from Buddhism to Taoism to Yoga—advocate balance. The twenty-first century is a stressful place for us and our children alike—as we run from tuition center to enrichment activities, our lives become crowded and stressful, like the congested roads we travel on and the traffic jams we get stuck in. We feel like we're never moving fast enough. Sometimes, perhaps, we need to stop the speeding car of twenty-first-century urban parenting and walk to a park so that we can breathe some fresh air, calm down, and re-center ourselves. We all need balance. Of course, we want our children to experience short-term success in their exams, but we also want them to be happy, healthy, and creative people who succeed in the long term, over the course of their lives.

HOW TO SUPPLEMENT YOUR CHILD'S EDUCATION

No school is perfect, and every school is inevitably a product of a particular culture and educational system. As a parent, you may want to understand the culture and context of your child's school by talking to teachers and other parents, and by paying close attention to what your child does in school. You can then figure out where the gaps are so that you can supplement appropriately.

If your child attends a progressive school that shuns more traditional approaches to learning and instead believes exclusively in discovery based learning, where students are expected to construct their own understanding of academic material, then you could supplement with more traditional academic work and practice sessions to ensure that your child receives a strong academic foundation. Conversely, if your child attends a school that focuses heavily on academic work and exam preparation, you could supplement with more open-ended, creative activities and conversations, and give your child time to play.

Supplementing a Progressive and Experimental Western Education

If your child attends a school with a Western-style approach to education of the type provided by many public and private schools in North America, state schools in the UK, or American or British international schools overseas, the school is probably doing a great job of getting your child to think creatively and express herself. She most likely gets lots of "real-world, hands-on experience" through projects and group work, and has plenty of time to play at school, as well as plenty of choices about how to spend her time and what to read or study. She is most likely encouraged to ask questions, challenge authority, and take intellectual risks. She is almost certainly encouraged to be extroverted and outgoing; a Western-style education places a premium on talking in class, sometimes to the detriment of quieter, more reflective students. Additionally, she probably engages in the arts on a regular basis.

However, the school may not be doing as good a job at ensuring that she masters crucial skills such as adding fractions, punctuating sentences correctly, and memorizing core content like the capitals of different countries or basic scientific facts. If your child's school rarely requires her to do individual work and instead encourages group activities and projects, she may not be learning how to focus her mind and concentrate in a more sustained academic way. Furthermore, if the school shuns any form of competition or stress (including exams), then she may not be learning how to push herself, cope with stress, or deal with failures and disappointments. And finally, if your child's school actively shuns homework and structured skill-building, she may not be spending enough time on building strong foundational skills and study habits. In this case, you could offer her a structured and disciplined home environment where she can study in traditional ways, and you may want to push her more at home.

Research suggests that Asian students in the West excel because their parents do a very good job of supplementing the creative education they get at school with a structured traditional education at home.[37] Furthermore, research suggests that most Asian parents supplement most intensively in the first ten years of a child's life. As the child progresses into middle school and high school, she is expected to be more independent. But in those first ten years, strong academic foundations are built, the ability to concentrate is honed, and excellent study habits are developed.[38]

What You Can Do:

■ **Provide regular math time**: Set times during the week where your child can work on her math skills using workbooks, online math sites, or puzzles/games. In his book *The One World Schoolhouse*, Salman Khan, founder of the Khan academy, warns parents and students of the dangers of "swiss-cheese learning" in math, arguing that gaps in students' learning *must* be repaired before they can move on to other concepts and topics. Since concepts in math build on each other in a fairly sequential, linear fashion, it is very important for students to have strong math foundations; studies of Asian-American students who are strong at math consistently

37 Barbara Schneider and Yongsook Lee, "A Model for Academic Success: The School and Home Environment of East Asian Students," *Anthropology & Education Quarterly* 21 (1990): 358–377. doi: 10.1525/aeq.1990.21.4.04x0596x

38 Ruth Chao and Vivian Tseng, "Parenting of Asians." In *Handbook of Parenting* vol. 4 ("Social Conditions and Applied Parenting"), ed. M. H. Bornstein (Mahwah, NJ: Lawrence Erlbaum Associates, 2002): 50–93.

reveal that their parents insist on supplementary practice with basic math skills, particularly during the elementary school years. Daily practice also helps children develop good study habits and extend their attention spans.

▪ **Provide daily reading and writing time**: Most progressive schools do a good job of encouraging free reading. This is something that you should reinforce at home on a daily basis. Progressive schools tend to fall short in grammar and punctuation instruction, overlooking it in favor of free, creative expression. While it's very important to encourage creative expression, all students also need to know basic grammar and punctuation rules such as how to use commas and semicolons appropriately. If your school doesn't teach grammar and punctuation, buy a good grammar book and teach your children yourself. There are also websites that help students learn basic grammar and punctuation. Find the resources and ensure that your child gets the practice he needs.

Recommended grammar resources:

English Brushup by John Langan and Janet Goldstein

For second-language learners: *English Grammar in Use* by Raymond Murphy

Online grammar games for young kids: http://www.sheppardsoftware.com/grammar/punctuation.htm

Grammar exercises for older kids: Towson University's Online Writing Support Program, http://www.towson.edu/ows/

Grammar Bytes (a wonderful grammar website): http://www.chompchomp.com/menu.htm

▪ **Help your child memorize core content**: For example, you may want to make him do basic map work and memorize the names of countries and capitals through games and puzzles. If there are content areas that, as a parent, you think are very important, such as specific historical events, you may want to expose him to these topics through nonfiction books, field trips, and even textbooks. There is so much information out there today that schools have a very hard time determining what students should learn, and often, in progressive schools, teachers feel content is far less important than skills. Instead of criticizing the school for not teaching kids about certain topics, you are better off identifying specific topics for your child to read about and study during vacation time. Studying, in its most traditional sense, involves reading material, taking notes on it, thinking about it, and committing key ideas and key bits of information to memory.

■ **Don't hesitate to use textbooks or workbooks for your child,** even if her school doesn't use or approve of them. Textbooks and workbooks are an excellent way of making sure that your child has a solid understanding of basic content and a solid grasp of basic skills. Most progressive schools prefer websites and online games to textbooks and workbooks, but for young children, textbooks and workbooks may be less distracting. In conversations with numerous parents whose children attend highly progressive Western schools, I have heard mothers say that they finally went out and bought a textbook and it helped their child a great deal.

■ **Limit the number of extracurricular activities that your child does**. While extracurricular activities such as sports and music are absolutely essential for a child's development, one or two are more than sufficient for most children. Too many parents feel compelled to enroll their children in a whole host of activities, leaving them overextended with not enough time to read, study, play, and relax. Encourage and value extracurricular activities, but make sure that your child is not overwhelmed by his extracurricular schedule. When I taught in the US, I was surprised at the number of hours that many of my students spent doing organized sports. Some were exhausted because they couldn't cope with the combination of long hours of sports practice, other activities, and homework. One high-school student I taught in New York would literally sleep through each school day because she was so exhausted from her swimming practices, which took place every morning as well as three evenings a week. Similarly, my high-school students in Singapore are often juggling numerous activities, and have little time to do their homework, read for pleasure, or relax with their friends. Even young kids are often overwhelmed by a slew of activities: music, sports teams, tae kwon do, art class, robotics, dance, etc. While each activity has value, overloading children with too many activities ends up being counterproductive. A child's physical and mental health depends on a balanced schedule and sufficient sleep.

■ **Don't worry so much about making everything "fun."** American education rhetoric is somewhat obsessed with making learning "fun." However, in my experience as an educator in the US and in Singapore, many students enjoy serious academic work, and parents shouldn't feel worried about encouraging students to engage seriously with challenging study. While some American education experts may say that all learning should be fun, I personally believe that the word "fun" is the wrong word to use. Learning should be challenging, meaningful, rigorous, engrossing, interesting, and satisfying. It does not need to be a game or a party. If your child attends a school that is focused on "fun," encourage serious learning activities at home to show him that earnest academic engagement can be pleasurable and satisfying. Eileen, a Chinese teacher at an international school, told me that she sees the Western emphasis on "fun" as one of the biggest differences between East and West. She added, "We Asians aren't so interested in constantly having fun. Our kids learn to like studying and learning. They don't expect or want everything to be a game or a party. As a result, they learn to extend their attention spans and develop their ability to concentrate."

Supplementing a Traditional Asian-style Education

If your child attends an exam- or results-oriented Asian school, the school is probably doing a great job of getting him to master crucial skills and memorize core content. He will almost certainly receive a very solid foundation in math, science and problem-solving. Additionally, attending academically oriented schools, doing homework, and revising for tests and exams will teach him excellent study skills and hone his powers of attention, focus, and concentration. He will not only develop a strong sense of self-discipline, but will also learn how to deal with stress and competition.

However, the school may not be doing so well at ensuring that he has the time, space, and freedom to think independently and creatively. In this case, you could offer him a relaxed home environment that encourages independent and creative thought. Many Asian parents find the demands of school are so crushing that there is little time for this kind of relaxed and fun supplementing, but try to remember the importance of critical and creative thought and make time for it whenever you can. Remember to step back from the rat race of exams and consider the ways you need to prepare your child for life.

Most importantly, make time for free play. When children are young, give them time to play in unstructured ways, without screens and gadgets. When children engage in imaginative play (let's make up our own restaurant, let's act out a story, let's play pirates, etc.), they're using their imaginations and developing their social skills. Many books have been written on the importance of play as fuel for the imagination. Don't tell your child what to play or how to play; let him decide for himself. Children need to be able to initiate and plan their own games so they get used to thinking for themselves and making independent decisions.

Recommended Books:

Play = Learning, by Kathy Hirsch Pasek

Einstein Never Used Flash Cards, by Kathy Hirsch-Pasek and Roberta Golinkoff

The Power of Play, by David Elkind

- **Make time for stories and free reading**: Read aloud to your child for pleasure, and encourage free reading for pleasure on a daily basis. Reading fiction engages the imagination and helps children develop empathy, among other benefits. Reading nonfiction helps children gain not just knowledge but also a sense of wonder and awe about the real world.

- **Encourage your child to write her own poems, short stories, and opinion pieces**. Don't worry about grammar and punctuation; just let her use her imagination and write what he wants. In my interviews with students in Singaporean schools, many said their teachers limited the topics they could write about in their compositions (love, rebellion, and death were off the table). Additionally, many parents and students described a "formula" for a high-scoring composition. To combat this formulaic approach to creative (or not so creative!) writing, encourage your child to stop feeling inhibited and take risks; encourage her to write whatever she wants and validate her original ideas and thoughts.

- **Encourage time outdoors and in nature**. In his wonderful book *Last Child In the Woods*, Richard Louv recommends a "green hour" for children every day, saying that an hour outdoors is crucial not just for a child's physical and mental health, but also for nurturing creativity. If you can't fit in a full hour of time in nature during the school week, give your child at least half an hour outside as a study break every evening, and then encourage him to spend more time outside on weekends and during school holidays. Ideally, time outside should be unstructured. Let him do whatever he wants—climb a tree, take a walk, sit by a pond and daydream, make mud pies, build a sandcastle, or catch some bugs.

- **Help your child explore nature on weekends and during holidays** by taking her to beaches, parks, nature trails/forests etc. These outdoor experiences provide wonderful opportunities for fun, hands-on education about the natural world.

- **Take your child to children's exhibits at museums,** or to concerts and theatre productions for children. This kind of low-stakes, hands-on learning is a wonderful complement to the high-stakes book learning that most students get in school.

- At mealtimes, bedtime, and during conversations, **encourage your children to ask questions about anything they're curious about**. You can do this by engaging them in a discussion of a book or any issue or topic, and then asking them what questions the discussion provoke in their minds. You might offer one of your own as a model. For example, when Lee Kuan Yew, the founding prime minister of Singapore, died, and the island responded with an outpouring of collective public grief, I asked my children what they wanted to know about him and his life. They were full of questions, ranging from "Why was he so famous?" to "Did he ever do anything bad or make mistakes?" to "What makes someone a great leader?"

  Kids naturally like to ask questions, so it's usually not hard to get them going. Such questions are a wonderful way to start deep and engaging conversations with your children. Talk to them about the importance of asking good questions. In life, coming up with the "correct answer" is often less important than being able to come up with the right questions. To balance out an exam system that is overly concerned with "correct answers," encourage your children to ask questions.

- **When you read books or discuss any topic with your children, ask them** *open-ended questions* (questions that don't have one right answer but instead invite multiple possibilities) to encourage divergent thinking. The problem with tests and exams is that they tend to reward convergent thinking and conformity, and they discourage children from generating a range of possibilities. Even well written and thoughtful exams tend to discourage experimentation and intellectual risk-taking.

Ask your children questions that require them to formulate an original opinion and to generate a range of possibilities. Don't expect a particular answer, but instead be open to whatever they say. The idea here is to get them to think for themselves and generate interesting possibilities.

Examples of open-ended questions:

- What do you think of this book? Why? (If the child hates the book, that's fine. This is one of the hardest things for me as an English teacher! When I love a book, I desperately want my students to love it too—but I have learned to honor opposing viewpoints. Everyone has a right to their own opinion of a book or a work of art, after all.)

- Do you think this character did the right thing? What could she have done differently? What would you have done in the same situation?

- What do you think this poem is really about?

- Are there other historical situations like this one? How are they similar or different?

- Did your friend do the right thing in this situation? What else could he have done? How else could he have handled the situation?

- Did this politician (or leader, or public figure) do the right thing in this situation? What else could she have done? What would you have done in this situation?

- What specific things do you think we can do to solve the problem of corruption (or garbage, pollution, environmental degradation, or any other problem you want) in our country?

- If you could change one thing about your school, what would it be?

- If you could change one thing about your country, what would it be?

▦ When your children come home from school, don't ask them what their test scores were. Instead, **ask them what they learned**. Focus on learning for its own sake so that your children begin to understand that learning has intrinsic value; it's not just about marks, scores, and exams. Ultimately, we want our children to develop a deep-seated love of learning, not just a single-minded desire to ace tests.

▦ And finally, **try to refrain from constantly telling your children what to do**. There is lots of value in getting a child to figure things out for himself. When my children are bored, I often say, "Boredom is fuel for the imagination. Use your own imagination and figure out what to do." If your child wants to draw a picture, don't tell her what to draw; let her decide for herself, and don't censor her choices. Allow and encourage her to have her own opinions and views. Give your children the space and time to think for themselves.

CHAPTER 5

Raising Resilient Children: How Do We Deal with Failure?

SUGARY CANDY OR HEALTHY (SOMETIMES BITTER) VEGETABLES?

Comment on report card from an international school: Molly would benefit from greater consistency with her homework. *What the teacher really means:* Molly has failed to submit two major assignments this term. She is disorganized and unmotivated, and she has no regard for deadlines. *Comment on paper in an American school:* Your paper would benefit from a more detailed exploration of the topic. *What the teacher really means:* Your paper is superficial and lacks substance and depth.

As a teacher in the US, I often felt nervous about critiquing my students' work in an honest fashion. I would try my hardest to be as positive as possible about every piece of writing that my students turned in. I worried immensely about their self-esteem: would honest criticism crush their sense of self? Would it inhibit them on future assignments and prevent them from taking intellectual risks or trying new things? Would it make them less motivated? How on earth do you tell a student that his ideas lack depth and originality without crushing him?

The private schools I worked at encouraged teachers to be as positive as possible when we wrote reports. (The public schools I worked at didn't require us to write anything at all; we just chose generic comments from a drop-down menu.) At one private school, teachers were instructed not to use the word "struggle" in reports because it sounded too negative. Instead of saying "When it comes to writing essays, Molly struggles to organize her ideas in a cohesive manner," we were told to say, "In her writing, Molly is developing her organizational skills." In another school, we were told not to criticize the child, but instead to rephrase every comment with a positive spin. Instead of saying, "Molly didn't turn in her report," we were urged to say, "Molly would benefit from spending more time on her homework."

After a decade of teaching in America, I perfected the art of "positive feedback," which I now liken to offering students a steady diet of sugary candy. Everything tastes sweet, and everyone's happy. But it might not be so good for the kids in the long run!

When I moved to Singapore, I had to readjust to South Asian and East Asian expectations for feedback and criticism. From my conversations with Asian moms, I've found that parents and students *want* real, honest, critical feedback. These parents don't want candy; they want vegetables—spinach- and broccoli-flavored feedback—and it's okay if the kids don't really like the taste. In fact, the bluntness and honesty of Asian mothers and teachers sometimes surprises me. At one parent-teacher conference, an Indian mother told me to "feel free to be strict with [her] son because he needs a firm hand." In a conversation with another mother, she told me that she often shouts at her son for doing "half-baked, rubbish work." These conversations stood in stark contrast to the "always be positive" mantra that I had repeatedly heard in the US.

Words like "awesome" and "great job" are not thrown around lightly in Singapore. While many of the students I interviewed from local Singaporean schools described the close relationships they had with their teachers, describing their teachers as "supportive" and "helpful," most agreed that Singaporean teachers are not in the business of praising children unless they really and truly deserve praise. In fact, it is often quite hard for children here to really please their teachers and parents. One mother I interviewed said, "My daughter's (Singaporean) piano teacher is never happy. No matter how much my daughter practices and how well she does, the teacher shouts at her and says, 'You can do better. *Aim higher.*'

The "aim higher" mantra is echoed in the media as well. Singaporeans are repeatedly exhorted to work harder and "not relax." In a *Straits Times* article,[39] education correspondent Sandra Davie reported that Singapore had the top problem-solving scores on the PISA test, and quoted the prime minister's comment on Facebook in response to this news: "It shows that we are on the right track, but I don't think we can afford to relax." This is the message that parents, educators, and students receive on a regular basis: *"We can't afford to relax. There is always more we can do to 'stay competitive.'"* Is this a good thing?

I struggle with these messages as a parent and an educator—sometimes the strong Singaporean sense of competition motivates me to work harder and push my own children and students more; at other times, I wonder whether all this rhetoric is just driving parents and educators towards a nervous breakdown. Yes, we should all aim higher, but can't we ever just take a breather and relax? Isn't some relaxation good and necessary? Are we burning ourselves and our children out too quickly, too young, too early?

When I arrived in Singapore, I was initially taken aback by the lack of sugar-coating that I encountered among parents. But surprisingly enough, my own children and the Asian children that I work with seem able to take this honest criticism. They don't collapse in tears or lose their sense of self-esteem; they just get serious and work harder. Ha-Young, a Korean-American student, told me, "Psychologically challenging experiences strengthen you. When my parents got angry at me for not doing excellent work, they used to

---

39 Sandra Davie, "Singapore Teens Rank #1 in Problem Solving," *The Straits Times*, April 2, 2014.

tell me that I'll thank them later. And I do thank them, because now I'm self-driven and strong."

Interestingly, though, American influence seems to be seeping into the Singaporean education system in many ways. While the brusque and honest nature of Asian-style feedback stands out to me, some Singaporeans seem to feel as though parents are becoming "too sensitive" and, as a result, children are "losing their way" and "behaving badly." In an editorial in the *Straits Times*, educator Ho Kong Loon writes, "In the end-of-term remarks, teachers circumnavigate the hassle of offending highly sensitive parents via the ingenious use of euphemisms. It is now considered taboo to use terms like naughty, inattentive, playful, lazy, quarrelsome, and so on."[40]

As a teacher, I've been working on being more honest with my feedback. Students benefit from honest feedback, and they need to

---

40 Ho Kong Loon, "Parents and Teachers Need to Work Together," *The Straits Times*, May 12, 2014.

ASIAN PARENTS SPEAK OUT

"Other mothers judge me negatively"

"My son Cayden does well at school, but my daughter Natalie is very different. She's more artistic, and she has a different kind of personality. She struggles with her academic work. Her self-esteem is particularly low because she compares herself to her brother, who has pleased everyone with his academic success.

I don't shout at her or punish her anymore when she gets bad grades, because she just freezes up and goes blank. She went through a phase of being really withdrawn and saying negative things about herself because she felt she couldn't live up to expectations. She still gets down about being in the bottom stream at school—she tells me the other kids make fun of her and she's already decided she's a dumbo. So I started to encourage her to do more art, because this is something she is good at and enjoys. And I tell her not to worry about her grades so much. But I can see that the other mothers judge me negatively for not pressuring my girl to do better in school. They think I'm not doing my job as a mother well."

—**Susan Chan**, mother of Cayden (twelve) and Natalie (nine)

be resilient enough to confront and accept criticism. Furthermore, their parents deserve to hear honest feedback on written reports. Yet my own instincts tend to be more sympathetic; I instinctively worry about a child's self-esteem and confidence. I often struggle to figure out where that line is: When am I being too indulgent? How demanding and critical should a teacher or parent be? Where's the line between motivating a child and shutting him down? When is pressure healthy and when does it become damaging? Should we always be pushing our children, or is it OK to give them some legitimate down time, some stress-free holidays, some feel-good praise, and some time for relaxation?

"AND WHAT DO YOU DO WHEN YOUR CHILD DOES BADLY ON A TEST?"

When I asked her how she responds to poor test scores, Min Li smiled and said, "I'll be honest. When my son gets a bad test score I have to take a moment to calm myself down. Then I try to speak to him about what went wrong without getting angry. But usually I lose my temper. I start shouting and I say things that really upset my husband, who is much more relaxed about all this than I am."

"What do you say?" I asked, curious.

"Well, I start yelling: do you want to be *a cleaner* when you grow up? Do you want to be *unemployed*? Do you know how competitive the world is? Do you know how important this is? And my husband doesn't like that. He says that I shouldn't devalue cleaners because all jobs have dignity. My husband is less results-oriented than I am. He says that as my son grows up, he will do better. My husband was careless as a child too, so he understands my son. My problem is that when I see a bad grade, I panic. I become so upset." I found Min Li's honesty both endearing and entertaining, particularly because she is such a soft-spoken and sweet person. I couldn't imagine her yelling at anyone.

When I asked another mother, Lei, how she dealt with bad grades, she said, "It depends on why the grade was bad. If my daughter does badly on a spelling test, I get angry. There is no excuse for that, because doing well on spelling is just a matter of studying. If you study hard enough, you should be able to get a perfect score. So if she doesn't get a perfect score, I tell her there is no excuse for laziness, and I will probably punish her by making her do many extra test papers and by taking away iPad and TV privileges for a week. On the other hand, if she does badly on a task that is more conceptual or creative, I don't get angry. I will sit with her and help her understand how she could have done better. For example, if she gets a word problem wrong on a math test because she really didn't understand it, then I will work with her on it and make her practice lots of similar problems. In these cases, it's not her fault, so it's not fair to get angry at her."

In some of my other interviews, Singaporean-Chinese mothers expressed concern about their children's self-esteem. Laura Tan, for instance, said, "I would never want my children to lose confidence in themselves. So if they fail, while I would tell them that they need to work harder, I would also try to take a step back and not focus on the failure so much. I would try to reset the system, so to speak, so that we can learn from mistakes without dwelling on the failure or disappointment." Laura went on to describe the benefits of failure, saying, "I think that it's okay for children to fail sometimes, because failure teaches humility. When we fail, we become more tolerant and less judgmental of others. And we learn how to recover from failure and move on. These are all important lessons."

In my interviews with Indian mothers, I encountered some healthy debate about the benefits and costs of being "failure averse" and "results oriented." In an impromptu chat over coffee one evening, Nandita, a strong and confident working mother with a ten-year-old daughter and a five-year-old son, said, "The problem with Indian mothers is that we tend to be too results oriented. When the child's performance starts to matter more than his feelings, then I think we have crossed the line." But Jhanvi, the mother of a ten-year-old, disagreed, saying, "Our children need to develop some emotional strength. If they make a mistake or don't do their best, they should be held accountable. In the real world, people don't worry so much about other people's feelings, and the fact of the matter is that the real world is performance oriented. If we mollycoddle our children, they won't have the emotional strength they need to face challenges when they grow up."

Sraboney, a liberal and thoughtful Indian mom, urged me to write this chapter, saying, "You've got to address the downside of a results-oriented culture. What are our children losing when we focus so much on marks, scores, grades, and competition? I am often asked if my daughter is in the advanced math class at her international school, and when I reply in the negative, I get a weird look from other Indian mothers. Why are we hell-bent on making our children geniuses? And for that matter, how do we decide that a child is superior to her peers? We mothers are so focused on test results, but are tests the true measure of a child's intellectual ability? We need to consider the costs of focusing so much on results and rankings."

WHAT THE KIDS SAY

In addition to talking to parents about these issues, I also asked some of my high school students how their parents reacted to low grades, and I got a number of interesting responses. Grace, a very smart and outspoken Chinese fourteen-year-old, said, "Nothing but perfection is acceptable in my home. If I come home with less than a perfect score, my parents get very angry. They want me to do well, and they are very invested in my learning. In contrast, when some of my Western friends do badly, their parents don't get upset. They say as long as the child did his best, that's all that matters. But in Chinese homes, doing your best is not enough. You have to deliver results." When I first asked her if she would be willing to share her experiences with me, she said, "If you want to know about strict Chinese parents, you're talking to the right person. My parents are very strict." Having taught Grace for a year, though, I can safely say that her parents' methods seem to have worked quite well: she is an extremely competent and conscientious student, and she engages enthusiastically in discussions.

Wang Fang, a diligent and thoughtful Chinese student who studied at an American school in Shanghai before moving to Singapore, said, "At my old school, some of my Western friends would get consolation treats from their parents when they did badly on tests. I couldn't believe it. They did badly on a test and their parents would feel bad for them, so their parents would take them out for pizza or ice cream to make them feel better. My parents were totally the opposite. If I did badly, they would get upset and say that I had to study harder."

Ha-Young, a highly successful Korean student who has attended international schools all her life, described how she once scored nine out of ten on a spelling test when she was in second grade. Her parents were extremely upset; after shouting at her, they ripped up the test, saying there was no excuse for losing a point. She said her parents expected nothing but the best from her at everything: academics, sports, any activity she participated in. "During summer vacation when I was young, I wasn't allowed out of my bedroom each morning until I had finished the pages of math problems that my parents had assigned. I had to study a lot as a child. My parents' standards were very high." When I asked Ha-Young whether she resented this pressure, she said that she resented it when she was young, but she now feels grateful for the intense discipline that her parents instilled in her early on. As a child, she said that she worked hard out of fear, but now she works hard for herself.

Another one of my Korean students, Seo-Yeon, described the testing frenzy that she encountered when she attended middle school in Seoul. She said that she and her peers experienced intense pressure to score well on exams, which were most often multiple choice. As soon as an exam would finish, the class leader would read the answers to the class so that students could check how many questions they had answered correctly and estimate their own scores. When they went home from school, the first thing their parents would ask them was "What did you get on the exam?" Seo-Yeon described the emphasis on perfect scores; "I remember once how I had studied hard and then I got one question on the exam wrong. My mother didn't get angry, but she shook her head and said that I hadn't worked hard enough. My studying wasn't sufficient. I remember feeling so sad." Despite taking a highly challenging set of IB courses, Seo-Yeon added that she found the academic demands at international school much easier than her old school in Seoul. "Other kids here who have only been exposed to Western education find the IB very stressful, but for me, it's quite easy compared to the pressure in Korea."

CONFLICTED, STRESSED, AND SEEKING BALANCE

Many mothers I've spoken to in Singapore are conflicted about how they should deal with their children's failures. They desperately want their children to succeed, and they often experience intense anxiety about their children's academic performances. As Fatima admitted to me, "I know I'm a *kiasu* mom because I feel more anxious than my son does when he takes an exam." A competitive society and a rapidly changing world make mothers anxious and more results focused than they would like to be.

Kavita, an Indian mother who recently moved away from Singapore, said that she was relieved to leave because she couldn't stand the pressure that she and her husband felt when they interacted with other Indian parents: everyone was completely obsessed with education and achievement. Kavita lamented, "At every party or social gathering, the main topic of conversation was school and academic achievement. Parents would endlessly discuss the level of competition or show off about their children's math scores. Or they would discuss tuition centers endlessly." Kavita has a dyslexic daughter who struggled with academic work at her school in Singapore. While she believed that her daughter would "find her own passions and discover her own magic," Kavita found herself becoming increasingly anxious when she interacted with other mothers. To add fuel to the fire, her husband became very tense at social events, and this strained their marriage immensely. As a result, Kavita pushed their daughter more than her instincts told her she should, and she simultaneously worried that she might be damaging her daughter's sense of self. She said that she was greatly relieved when she could finally extricate herself from Singapore's pressure-cooker approach to education and parenting. "When my husband's contract here came to an end and we were able to leave, I felt like I could breathe again."

FAILURE AND FEAR IN THE TWENTY-FIRST CENTURY

Asian parents in the twenty-first century are certainly an anxious lot. They believe deeply that educational success is the first step to having a good career and being financially secure in the future. Much of this anxiety comes from the incredibly rapid rate of change that Asians have experienced in the last three decades.

In just one generation, Singapore transformed from a developing country with low literacy and health indicators to a high-performing developed nation with a highly literate and healthy population. Both India and China have opened up their economies and seen high levels of growth over the last two decades. In 1976, China was battered by the effects of the Cultural Revolution; a whole generation of children had been denied access to education. Yet in 2013, less than forty years later, China has morphed into an extraordinarily powerful nation, and children in Shanghai score amongst the top in the world in international tests like the PISA and the TIMMS. East Asians are well aware of their educational prowess, and young Chinese, Singaporean, Korean, and Japanese children are increasingly ambitious and confident.

While India's public (government-run) educational system still suffers from poor-quality schools that lack qualified teachers and adequate resources, the middle and upper classes have benefited from the liberalization of the economy; these relatively affluent children now have far better economic prospects than the older generation had. In the last decade, a number of fancy new international schools have sprouted all across India, promising affluent Indian children a world-class education. Importantly, middle- and upper-class Indian children now grow up feeling confident that they, too, can compete on a global stage. The high degree of confidence that my students from India exhibit in the classroom contrasts with the intimidation I felt as a teenager when I left India for the US and was faced with the overwhelming confidence of my American peers. Middle- and upper-class Indian kids today benefit from a new set of messages about their capabilities: they see a wide range of smart and capable Indians succeeding in the global marketplace, so they fully believe that they, too, can rise to the top in a global setting. Students across Asia today not only have far greater exposure to the world than their parents ever had, thanks to modern media, but also live in societies that are free from the subjugation of colonial rule (in India and Singapore) or Maoist rule (in China). Asians now feel as though they are equal competitors on the world stage. Asian parents want to make sure that their children don't feel inferior or subservient to anyone; they are highly ambitious for their children, and they are trying their very best to prepare them to compete in the twenty-first century. All this ambition and competition has its costs, however.

FIXED MINDSETS VERSUS GROWTH MINDSETS

We all want our children to feel successful and confident, and we all want to see them succeed. Given these desires, our intuition as parents often urges us to protect our children from failure and mistakes. Contemporary research says this is not the right approach.

Failure can be a healthy experience for children if it is framed as a learning experience. While we may hate to think about it, the fact of the matter is that all our children will inevitably experience some failures in their lives. No one is completely immune to failure, and all great risks and ideas are accompanied by a very real chance of failure. The key to success is not to avoid failures (or not take risks), but rather to deal effectively with failures, setbacks, and disappointments. Research suggests that if a child is able to pick herself up, be resilient, and persevere despite a setback or failure, she will have a much better chance at long-term success than a student who simply avoids taking any risks that may lead him to fail.[41] In fact, I sometimes worry about my super-talented students who never seem to fail at anything. If they don't have some practice developing resilience in school, how will they deal with the inevitable failures that they will experience in adult society? Low-stakes failures in school can actually be a healthy experience for children in the sense that they learn that failing at something is not the end of the world. They can develop skills such as resilience, perseverance, and humility.

Our instincts as parents might also be to praise our children. "You're so smart!" might seem like the right way to help them build their confidence. However, recent research suggests that too much praise can actually be damaging, especially if kids are praised in the wrong way. Research by Carol Dweck, a Stanford psychologist who writes widely on the effects of various kinds of praise, suggests that children should always be praised for their *efforts,* not for their results or abilities. Dweck connects the issue of dealing with failure to her belief that children have either a "growth mindset" or a "fixed mindset." She outlines the basic characteristics of each as follows:

Growth mindset
- The child does not see his abilities as fixed or innate; he believes that he can do better by working harder.
- The child believes her abilities and talents can be cultivated through hard work.
- The child is ready to take intellectual risks and learn.
- The child is open to constructive criticism and advice.
- The child is not afraid of failing, but sees failure as part of the learning process.

---

41 Carol Dweck, *Mindset: The New Psychology of Success* (New York: Random House, 2006): 174–192.

- The child believes that effort, hard work, and persistence will eventually pay off; failure is a learning experience that will help him on the road to success.

Fixed mindset
- The child sees herself as having certain talents or abilities that are fixed.
- The child does everything possible to present a positive image of himself.
- The child sees failure as a direct reflection of her own abilities.
- The child is afraid to take intellectual risks because failure could potentially damage how he sees himself or how others see him.
- The child gets upset and angry when offered constructive criticism or advice.
- The child is afraid of taking any kind of risk, intellectual or otherwise, because he is so afraid of failing.

It's not hard to see that a growth mindset will take one further in life than a fixed mindset will. How, then, can we encourage a growth mindset in our children?

The first part of developing a growth mindset is to emphasize hard work over ability. Research suggests that this is a fundamental aspect of Asian culture, particularly East Asian culture. Jin Li, professor of education at Brown University and author of *Cultural Foundations of Learning*, asserts that Asian parents tend to believe more in nurture than in nature, or in other words, they value effort over ability. Chinese parents, she writes, stress the importance of *practice*, *struggle*, and *diligence* in the learning process. When a student does badly, she is urged to work harder and practice more, because Chinese parents believe that this is the way to overcome any obstacle. In her chapter "Mind and Virtue Learning Processes," Li writes that the ideal Chinese learner sees lack of ability as a "hardship" (ku) that must be confronted and overcome. "Instead of giving up, one will spend more time, seek more help, and practice more." She offers readers common Chinese expressions that stress emphasis on perseverance: "Utmost sincerity can break stone," and "Keep on carving unflaggingly, and metal and stone will be engraved."[42]

In my conversations with Asian mothers, I heard echoes of Jin Li's assertions. One mother said, "Children need to know that practice and hard work will ultimately get them where they want to go." Another mother said, "Excelling at math is all about practice." A third mother said, "When my son does badly in school, I tell him he needs to work harder. If he says he is not capable, I get angry. Anyone can do well if they put their mind to it and dedicate themselves to their studies."

Ironically, while Asians clearly *help* their children develop growth mindsets by emphasizing effort and practice, they may simultaneously *prevent* children from developing a growth mindset by overemphasizing results and making a child feel bad if she fails to deliver the expected results. In a system where primary-school children, beginning in first or second grade, take ninety-minute exams on which "every mark counts" in all their major subjects at the end of each semester, children become very focused on results and very averse to failure. Competitive exam systems can lead Asian parents to focus on rankings, marks, and scores to the exclusion of all else. But all children cannot possibly be at the top of the class, and often, even with maximum effort, a child may not do as well as he would like.

What happens when parents berate children for bad results, even when they have tried their hardest? What is the message that the parent is sending? What are the effects? Does a child's fear of not delivering the expected results ultimately translate into strength, or does it create an inhibited and fearful person in the long run?

The only certainty in all this is that everyone *will* experience failure at some point in their lives. No human is exempt from the feeling of being inadequate in some way or another, and no one is uniformly successful all the time. We can try to protect our children

---

42 Jin Li, *Cultural Foundations of Learning*: 139, 143.

from failure when they're young, but—as painful as it may be to think about—they will all experience their share of failures as they grow older. (It is important to note that different students and parents define failure in different ways: some students think of a B+ as a terrible failure, while others are fairly content with a C.) Failure to meet expectations, disappointments, and rejection are as much a part of human life as success and acceptance are. While telling a child "failure is not an option" may produce results in the short run, it can be debilitating in the long run, because it can prevent her from taking healthy risks and living a full life.

My personal view on this front is that **failure should always be an option**. Children should always know that they may fall short of expectations and that that is okay. Allowing them to fail does not mean lowering expectations; they should not fail because they are lazy or unmotivated. However, children should be encouraged to try something new, select a more difficult topic, present an original or controversial view, accept an academic or extracurricular challenge, or compete in an area where they may lose. They should be encouraged to experiment with ideas and writing styles, to try a different method of solving a math problem, to voice a contrary opinion in an academic discussion, and to audition for the school play or try out for the school sports team. If they do end up disappointed, they should be taught to pick themselves up again and move forward. It is through the experience of taking risks, struggling, and failing, that children will develop resilience and really learn. In fact, with my own children, I often say, "A better word for failure is a learning experience." I know in my own life that I have learned far more from my failures than I have from my successes.

When he was in second grade, my son ran for student council and lost. He came home agitated and upset by the loss, complaining bitterly about how "unfair" everything was. He ran again in the first semester of third grade and lost again, and came storming home, angry, tearful, and resentful. He sulked for a few hours, indulged in some self-pity, told me I didn't understand anything, and then eventually got over the loss and proceeded to get on with things.

Each time he lost, I praised him for having the courage to make a speech in front of his classmates and take the risk of running for a leadership position. I also talked to him about the importance of losing graciously and being persistent.

Later in his third-grade year, he had another opportunity to run for student council. He practiced his speech more this time round, and he was finally elected to the position. This time, he came bounding through the door, full of excitement and pride, as he high-fived me and regaled me with stories of his great success. Both my husband and I congratulated him on persisting and trying again. It took him three tries to make it onto the student council, but I think that in many ways he learned much more from trying repeatedly than he would have from winning on his first attempt.

AMERICAN PARENTS AND THE RHETORIC OF VICTIMIZATION

The attitude of American parents, at least as it is reflected in American parenting and education literature, appears to be significantly different from that of their Asian counterparts in terms of the messages they give their children. While diligence is viewed as a very positive trait by Asian parents, many Americans tend to feel more ambivalent about the word. In her book *A is for Admission: The Insider's Guide for Getting into the Ivy League and Other Top Colleges,* college counselor Michele A. Hernandez, who used to head the admissions office at Dartmouth College, urges teachers *not* to say that a student is diligent in a recommendation letter. She writes, "I want to add a note about teachers who use words like "diligent" and "conscientious" [in their recommendations]…admissions officers at highly selective colleges [in the US] tend to interpret words like these to mean that the student is merely a hard worker, or a grind, but not a very insightful or naturally bright student."

In my experience, American educators often associate diligence, drills, practice, and discipline with kids who are boring and uncreative; the phrase "drill and kill" says it all. High-achieving American kids are somehow supposed to have great academic results without putting in the hard yards. They need to convince college officials that they are *not* "workhorses" or "nerds" who stay up late at night studying for tests, but naturally gifted students who achieve stellar academic results without actually working too hard. Devaluing hard work, effort, and diligence in favor of "natural ability" "talents," and "passion" could contribute to a child developing a fixed mindset—the conviction that she has a set ability and can't improve with effort.

Interestingly, contemporary education rhetoric in America asserts that a child's failure to perform academically is a reflection of the *setting* being inadequate. While I have worked with Western parents who hold their children accountable for their performance, I have also witnessed parents and teachers making excuses for children instead. For example, in a parent-teacher meeting I once had, instead of acknowledging that his son wasn't doing the required reading, the father, distraught and defensive, said, "Well, my son has had a really rough time these last few months. He's had issues with his friends that have made him upset. And he doesn't really like the book that the class is studying." This particular father believed that altering external factors such as the curriculum or the child's peer group would be more beneficial than making his son work harder.

ASIAN PARENTS SPEAK OUT

"Questioning an adult is seen as disrespectful"

"My daughter was taking a test. She noticed an error in the test—one of the sentences just didn't make sense. So she put her hand up to ask the teacher about it. The teacher ordered her to put her hand down—no questions allowed during a test. When my daughter came home and showed me the test, I could see the error. I could see why she was confused and unsettled by it. I wish the teacher had let her ask the question. Our children are often taught not to ask questions because questioning an adult is seen as disrespectful. I would never want my girls to be disrespectful, but asking a legitimate question is not a form of disrespect. I want them to feel comfortable asking questions."

—**Faith Lee**, mother of Sophia (eight) and Lily (six)

Or perhaps he wasn't sure *how* to make his son do the required homework. In a youth-centered society where children are increasingly empowered, some parents don't actually have the authority to tell their children to get down to work.

American books on parenting and education reinforce this perspective on struggling or failing children. They place the responsibility for a child's success or failures on the shoulders of the teachers and the environment instead of holding the child accountable. In her interesting and insightful book *What's Math Got to Do with It?* Stanford professor Jo Boaler presents three case studies of children who were struggling with math in school. The first is titled "Jorge, Who Needed a Chance and an Opportunity"; the second is "Rebecca, Who Needed to Understand"; and the third is "Alonzo, Who Needed to Use His Ideas."[43] Boaler provides highly sympathetic portrayals of how these children were not learning math because their teachers were not engaging enough and their math classes were not relevant and hands-on. As I read these sections, I couldn't help imagining the stereotypical Asian-mom response to these children: "Jorge, Who Needed to Work Harder"; "Rebecca, Who Needed to Work Harder"; and "Alonzo, Who Needed to Work Harder." This unsympathetic Asian response would be politically incorrect in the West, since the dominant discourse presented in Western books and websites on education and parenting rarely holds the child accountable for anything. Even privileged children are often written about as if they are victims who need to be rescued from boring and outdated pedagogical techniques or from insipid and insensitive adults.

Although American parents and teachers may be far more indulgent than their Asian counterparts, American teachers and schools do have a distinct advantage when it comes to encouraging creativity and innovation in their classrooms. American teachers typically encourage more intellectual risk-taking because they are not as

---

43 Jo Boaler, *What's Math Got to do With It?* (New York: Penguin Books, 2009): 161–170.

constrained by external exams or as driven by a societal emphasis on results. In fact, many children's books and children's television shows focus on a "Yes, we can" message: from *The Little Engine That Could* to *Handy Manny* to *Dora the Explorer*, American children are often told that they can do anything they want. They are encouraged to take risks, try new things, have their voices heard, formulate original opinions, and be different, and they are provided with low-fear, low-stakes environments where they *can* take risks and experiment. So, while devaluing effort may contribute to a fixed mindset, encouraging risk-taking and accepting failure may contribute to a growth mindset. In many ways, building a child's confidence and protecting him from a debilitating fear of failure may be at least as important, if not more important, than pushing him to work harder and achieve top scores.

One of the things I loved about teaching in the US was the tremendous freedom and autonomy that teachers have in the classroom. This was true in both the private schools and public schools where I worked. When my husband attended graduate school at Dartmouth, I taught at the local public high school in Hanover, New Hampshire, for two years. Though it was a public school, I had almost unlimited freedom to design my own units, assessments, and activities without the constraints of external exam systems. My colleagues and I could teach what we were most passionate about; we could experiment with texts, ideas, and activities; and we could offer our students a range of creative ways to explore ideas and take intellectual risks. Students who chose original approaches to a project or assignment were lauded and celebrated.

With the introduction of the Common Core, a set of standards in math and English that dictate what students should know and be capable of at the end of each grade, the US seems to be moving toward a standardized, prescriptive curriculum akin to the national education systems in Asian and European countries. However, as the Common Core prescribes only learning goals but not specific texts, pedagogies, or high-stakes national exams, it still offers educators far more freedom and autonomy than systems in Asia do.

While American parents and educators may send mixed messages to children about the value of good old-fashioned hard work and diligence, they tend to do a better job of lowering the educational stakes and allowing children to take risks.

In an ideal world, Asian and American parents would learn from one another and create a balance: celebrating diligence, emphasizing effort, holding children accountable, but simultaneously offering them the freedom to take risks and be original without having to worry so much about results.

SELF-ESTEEM AND HAPPINESS: Is effort always enough?

Most of the parents I spoke with in Singapore believed firmly that self-esteem is *not* something that a parent or teacher can just give a child. They all stressed, in one way or another, that self-esteem is the product of hard work and earned success. When a student works hard, masters a skill, and does well in school, she will feel competent and confident. It is this sense of competence and confidence that will build self-esteem.

Yet there are children who, despite all their hard work, still don't do as well as they would like. How do these particular kids feel about themselves? How do we help them feel secure about themselves? And what about students who excel—are their results purely due to effort, or do they arise from a student's innate talents?

Every year, I encounter a few students who have particularly impressive minds, and I find myself watching these kids with wonder and admiration. While they have a lot to learn—they are, after all, still young—it is easy to recognize and admire their intellectual firepower as they wrestle with texts and ideas, as they strive to express what they feel and understand in words, as they argue and defend their opinions. I often wonder what it is that creates a brilliant mind. Is it all in the genes? Is it a delicate intertwining of nature and nurture? How much does environment affect intellectual development?

While it is very hard to separate the effects of nature (genes) from nurture (environment and effort), a wide range of studies show that a substantial part of a student's IQ or academic ability stems from the genes.[44] In fact, in her book *Born Together, Reared Apart*, Nancy Segal presents the intriguing results of studies done on identical twins who were separated at birth, showing that over half the variance in many personality traits and mental abilities can be explained by genetic factors and attributed to heredity as opposed to the environment.[45] While I have no doubt that genes influence our abilities, I have also read many interesting books on neuroplasticity and the way our brains are shaped by our experiences and environments, leading me to believe that **excellence in any field (academic or non-academic) tends to be a function of sustained effort over time**. In other words, a student who has been immersed in a language-rich environment since birth and has read extensively all through her elementary years will be far more likely to excel in English in high school than a student who didn't read much in the early years.

Similarly, a student who has spent time on math every day since she was four will be far better equipped to do high school math as a teenager. When I asked my Korean student Ha Young whether she thought she was "naturally talented" at math, she replied, "Well, I've just done so much math that all that practice has made me good at it. I think it's hard to know whether I have any natural talent. All I do know is that math is very easy for me because I spent so much time as a young child practicing, and I have always spent time on math." Similarly, when I think of my English superstar students, it is hard to say they are "naturally talented"; they have benefitted from hours and hours of reading and language exposure over the first fifteen years of their lives. Just as excelling in a field may be partially due to genes and partially due to sustained exposure and effort in that area over time, struggling in a field may also be due both to genes and a lack of sustained exposure and effort in that field over time.

---

44 Arthur W. Toga and Paul M. Thompson, "Genetics of Brain Structure and Intelligence," *Annual Review of Neuroscience* 28 (2005): 1–23.

45 Nancy Segal, *Born Together, Reared Apart* (Cambridge, MA: Harvard University Press, 2012).

So I have a confession to make: I'm a terrible, horrible driver. It took me years to get a driving license; in fact, my entire family was amazed when I finally passed my test. My inability to drive well has always been a source of humiliation and frustration for me, and it has limited me in many ways. Fortunately for me, driving and the skills that accompany it (visual-spatial skills, motor coordination) have never been part of academic curricula, so my weaknesses in this area have never hindered my academic career. I've often wondered, though, how different my life would be if these skills—driving, visual-spatial skills, motor coordination—had been tested and valued in schools. I would have been miserable. I would have been placed in remedial classes, and I would have felt like a total failure.

I make this confession to demonstrate a fact: sometimes there are skills that a student is just plain weak at. While abilities can be cultivated, sometimes that cultivation requires substantial strain and struggle, and even with maximum effort, the results do not match expectations. Also, often the cultivation (or intervention) has to start early to be effective. Over my fifteen years of teaching English, I've found that some high-school students don't intuitively understand how language works, and they make all kinds of weird and awkward grammatical errors because they don't have an ear for language. This could be because they didn't read enough as young children, or because their brains are less wired to understand and use language—or, most likely, a combination of the two. Similarly, some students find it very difficult to think abstractly and analytically; they just don't get the subtext in a work of literature, and they have a very hard time making inferences. Again, this could be because they haven't read enough and discussed complex ideas enough in elementary and middle school, or it could be that their brains haven't yet made that cognitive leap from concrete thinking to abstract thinking, or a combination of the two. Either way, they struggle with the task of literary analysis at the high-school level.

Now, all these students can get much better with practice (as I did with driving), and with regular work, they will eventually be able to pass the required exams and achieve a certain baseline level of competency (as I did when I finally got my license), but the fact is that school probably makes them feel pretty lousy about themselves. Berating, pressuring, and punishing these students for poor performances, especially when they are trying their best, is not going to serve any purpose. All it will do is further damage their self-esteem. I feel strongly that struggling students who are clearly working hard should be commended for their diligence and improvement, and encouraged by both teachers and parents; unrealistic expectations and extreme pressure can do a lot of damage.

Most Asian parents I have worked with seem quite balanced in their approach to their children's academic performance. Most mothers I interviewed gave me the impression that they pushed their children, but not beyond their limits, and they tempered pressure with unconditional love and affection. Unfortunately, not all parents are like this, and even those who are cannot always prevent their children from crumbling under the pressure of society's expectations. Asia abounds with stories of students killing themselves because they didn't pass exams or students sinking into depression because they feel inadequate academically. Even high-performing students can become suicidal because, despite their efforts and achievements, they haven't attained the impossibly high scores they need to make it into the college of their choice. They feel they have let their parents down and have been judged and evaluated negatively by society. When any society makes students feel so bad about themselves that they actually contemplate suicide, it has clearly crossed a line in the most egregious and upsetting manner. We need to protect our children from ever believing that their self-worth is dependent on their academic performance.

PAYING THE ULTIMATE PRICE: Student suicides

In September 2012, *The Asian Parent* magazine reported that in a study of over 600 Singapore children between the ages of six and twelve, 22 percent indicated that they wanted to kill themselves or had harbored thoughts of killing themselves. Many children cited academic stress, the "fear of examinations," and low scores on exams as reasons for contemplating suicide. (The test involved a self-administered rating scale.)[46] Doctors Alvin Liew, Choon Guan Lim, and Daniel Fung from the Institute of Mental Health in Singapore conducted the study, titled "Suicidal Behavior in Children and Adolescents–Prevalence and Risk Factors." *The Asian Parent* went on to report that the results are not surprising given that the most common cause of death amongst Singapore youths, besides accidents, is suicide. Across Asia, too, suicide rates among students and young adults are disproportionately high. This is often attributed to the degree of pressure and competition that so many young Asians feel.

As parents and educators, we have a tremendous role to play in the physical and emotional safety of our children. We need to recognize when a child is being pushed beyond her breaking point, or when her self-esteem and sense of purpose are severely damaged. Demanding excellence of a child and pushing students to do their best are laudable, but as parents and educators, we have to know our kids and know where the line is. Ultimately, a child's sense of self matters far, far more than a grade or score.

ACHIEVING BALANCE: The parenting seesaw

It's interesting that all children, whether they are toddlers or teens, tend to simultaneously need opposing forms of help and support. For example, while they need structure and predictability, they also need a considerable amount of freedom. Without structure, there's chaos and they tend to flounder; yet without freedom, creativity and imagination are stifled.

Similarly, children need high expectations and some pressure or stress so that they really push themselves, but they also need a safe and nurturing environment where they feel comfortable taking risks and failing.

---

46 "Child Suicide amongst Singapore Kids," *The Asian Parent*, September 25, 2012, http://sg.theasianparent.com/singapore_children_suicide_depression/

They need guidance because they are too young and inexperienced to make good choices on their own, but at the same time they also need to be given choices and left to themselves so they think creatively and learn to make their own decisions.

They need teachers and parents who are simultaneously firm and nurturing, who are at once both "hands-on" and "hands-off."

Here are some research-backed suggestions to help you guide and empower your children as you walk that tricky balancing beam, finding your footing and keeping yourself steady as a parent.

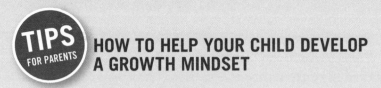

HOW TO HELP YOUR CHILD DEVELOP A GROWTH MINDSET

How does a parent or educator help a child develop a growth mindset, ensuring she values effort and develops persistence and resilience?

Here are some suggestions adapted from Carol Dweck's *Mindset*:

1. **Praise effort, not ability.** For example, don't tell your child that he's a fantastic writer. Instead, praise the time and energy he put into the writing process and the specific techniques that he used. Say, "You worked really hard on this piece of writing, and your hard work paid off. Your description of the dragon is full of interesting details; I particularly loved how you described his tail."

   Similarly, don't tell your child that she's a "gifted mathematician." Instead, say, "I like how you solved this difficult problem by writing all your steps down so carefully. You really thought hard about it."

2. **Don't tell your kids they are smart.** Tell them that if they work hard enough at anything, they'll do well. **Always send the message that hard work, effort, and persistence are the keys to success.**

3. **Think carefully about how you frame failure.** It's not a bad thing. In fact, it's good for kids to fail sometimes; it teaches them that failure is not the end of the world and helps them develop resilience. Don't protect your kids from failure. Instead, when they do fail, **help them reframe their failures as learning experiences**. Tell them that everyone encounters failure at some point. Strong, successful people don't fall apart or get down on themselves for failing; they *learn* from their failures.

   When your child comes home with a low grade on a test, don't dwell on the low grade. Instead, discuss how he can do better next time. Ask questions, such as: What strategies can you use? How can you work harder? What can you learn from this experience so that you do better next time?

4. **Encourage intellectual risks.** Encourage your child to tackle the harder topic or take the harder course. Encourage her to try out for student council or audition for a role in the school play. Tell her that you value risk-taking ability and the desire to try more than her final grade. What matters most is that she is willing to take a

risk and try something challenging. Praise initiative and risk-taking along with effort. These are crucial qualities for a growth mindset.

5. **Focus on learning, not results:** When your child comes home from school, don't immediately ask him what he got on his math test. Instead, ask him what he learned at school and discuss the learning that occurred.

6. **Emphasize that learning is not easy, but it is satisfying and pleasurable.** Help your child understand that learning is fulfilling for its own sake, not just for the sake of a grade, and overcoming challenges through hard work makes learning *more* satisfying and rewarding.

The ultimate goal of education should be to inspire a child with a **genuine love of learning**. If you can help your child understand the joy and satisfaction that a cerebral life can provide, then he will seek knowledge of his own accord. As parents and educators, our goal is not to convince our children that they are smart; it is to show them that learning is exciting and satisfying. Light the proverbial fire, and the child will do the rest.

HOW TO KNOW YOUR CHILD

Finding fulfillment: The why and how of knowing your child

"I have seen so many children pushed and coached to get into gifted programs, and many of these children can't take the pressure. While every society needs accelerated programs to meet the needs of gifted and high-ability children, these highly academic programs are not for all kids, and parents need to be aware of this," says Clarinda Choh, the head of the gifted education program at Hwa Chong Institution. She adds, "Too many Asian parents buy into a one-dimensional, narrow definition of success and force their children to conform to it, causing their children and themselves great stress and unhappiness. This does not bring happiness; instead it makes a person feel inadequate and miserable. In contrast, studying a subject you love and pursuing a career you enjoy bring tremendous satisfaction and fulfillment."

What does it mean to "know" your own child? It means being able to listen to her, instead of just telling her what to do. It also means understanding her strengths and passions, and encouraging her to reflect upon her own strengths.

The following techniques can help parents understand their children:

- **Watch how your child plays**: A child's natural inclinations during times of free play reveal a lot about what he enjoys most. Some children naturally gravitate toward building activities, while others prefer art or books. These choices will convey a child's natural interests and proclivities quite clearly, and often quite early.

- **Offer your child free time to do what she wants**: These choices will help a child decide what he enjoys doing.

- **Ask your child what subjects, books, and activities he enjoys**. Such conversations can help you understand your child better and will help him understand himself better.

- **Be open to different subjects and interests**: If your child loves art, don't dismiss this interest and wish that she loved physics instead. One Chinese teacher I interviewed told me, "every Chinese mom's worst nightmare is that her child will decide to be an artist." But in the visual- and design-oriented twenty-first century, students of art have many wonderful career options, including graphic design, interior design, advertising, and photography. If nothing else, your child may find a hobby that will sustain her through her life. Accept who she is, and make sure she knows that you love and accept her.

- **Realize that learning disabilities are *not* a myth**: Children may be born with a learning disability such as dyslexia, and there are students who legitimately suffer from attention problems, a lack of working memory, limited visual-spatial skills etc. These learning issues are not myths, and they are not a form of "laziness." While Americans are sometimes too quick to test, diagnose, and label children, Asian parents seem to have the opposite issue. They see these American trends of testing and labeling as "excuse-making." While I would never advocate using a label to excuse a child from working hard and trying his very best, I sometimes worry that some Asian parents automatically brand struggling children as "lazy."

If, despite his best intentions, your child is struggling to read or focus, you might need to determine what the underlying problem is. Support him by talking to his teachers and getting him extra help.

If the learning issue seems severe, see a specialist who can diagnose it and offer specific strategies to help him. Not every child is cut out for intense academic work, and that's okay. Find your child's strengths and support him as much as possible in those areas.

- **Encourage your children to be reflective**: Self-knowledge and introspection are very important qualities, and children should be encouraged to develop a deep knowledge of their own personalities, interests, strengths, and learning preferences.

PART 3

MYTH, MEDIA AND METAPHOR

The Stories We Tell and the Language We Use

"The human mind thinks in metaphors and learns through stories"

—Mary Catherine Bateson

CHAPTER 6

Myth and Media:
The Stories We Tell and the Scripts They Give Us

A BOLLYWOOD MOMENT

Over the weekend, I watched an old Bollywood movie called *Kal Ho Naa Ho,* which literally translates as "Whether or Not Tomorrow Comes." In the movie, the hero, played by Indian heartthrob Shah Rukh Khan, is a young man who is dying of a heart condition. Keeping his medical condition a secret, he finds pleasure in helping others around him. As the movie progresses, he falls in love with a young woman. Knowing that he doesn't have much time to live, however, he doesn't pursue her; instead, he sets her up with his best friend, who is also in love with her.

As I watched Shah Rukh Khan sing, dance, and cry his way through the movie, I was struck by the role that the older generation played in the story. The three main characters were supposed to be in their twenties. As they deal with love and loss, hope and heartbreak, all three of them turn to their parents and grandparents for help, advice, and support. The wedding song and dance sequence (all but inevitable in Bollywood movies) includes old grandparents, overweight mothers, and balding fathers dancing with the hot Bollywood stars. KHNH, as the movie is fondly called in India, is not unique in featuring mothers, fathers, and grandmothers so prominently. Most Bollywood movies have a host of older characters who the heroes and heroines turn to for support, guidance, and advice at some point in the movie.

Perhaps the presence of the older generation struck me as particularly interesting because it presented such a contrast to what one sees in Hollywood movies. In Western media, independent adult characters rarely turn to their elders for help. They are much more likely to rely entirely on themselves or seek help from their peers. The image of a grown man turning to his mother or grandmother for comfort would be not just unusual but even unsettling for a Western audience. In contrast, Shah Rukh, the king of Bollywood for the last twenty years, routinely cries in his mother's arms and seeks blessings from his grandmother in a wide range of movies. Indian audiences find these scenes comforting and moving; the role of the extended family is firmly entrenched in almost all Indian scripts.

While neither Hollywood nor Bollywood reflects reality, they both reveal something about what their respective societies value or idealize. Bollywood tends to romanticize the family unit, while Hollywood tends to idealize individualism. No surprise there—these industries originate within particular cultural contexts, after all.

AUNTIE–UNCLE CULTURES IN ASIA

Watching KHNH and thinking about the idealization of family made me think more deeply about the relationship between generations in the East. When I arrived in Singapore, I remember being momentarily disarmed and surprised by the fact that every adult, from the taxi drivers to the old couple living next door, was an "auntie" or an "uncle."

"Just like back home," I thought. "Just like India."

Across the East, children are taught the tremendous importance of addressing an elder appropriately. Never, ever, ever "take the name" of an elder, we were told when we were kids. We had specific words to address our actual relatives and we called all non-related adults "auntie" or "uncle."

What does it mean for a child to use such names for every non-related adult? To start with, the terms imply a familial relationship, suggesting that adults must treat all children as if they are part of the same family. In other words, all adults need to work together to raise children. Likewise, children need to respect and obey all the adults they encounter, as they would their own family members.

These terms originate from a community orientation. Historically, most Asians were raised in strong communities: in Singapore, kids grew up in communal villages; in India and China, they grew up in large joint-families with three generations living together under one roof. While Asia has industrialized rapidly over the last fifty years, it is still attached, at least in theory, to the ideals of community, extended family networks, and communal child-rearing.

In traditional societies, all the adults in a community or tribe are responsible for the well-being and socialization of the younger generation. In his book *The World Until Yesterday: What Can We Learn from Traditional Societies?*, Pulitzer Prize winner Jared Diamond describes the benefits of "allo-parenting," or communal

ASIAN PARENTS SPEAK OUT

"You must be respectful to your auntie"

"I came home one day and heard my daughter Alicia ordering our helper to get her a snack and to clean up some food that had been dropped on the floor. I was furious. I told her she was never to speak like that to the helper again. 'You are only seven.' I told her. 'Auntie is much older than you. And you must be respectful to your auntie. She is here to help us, and we must be kind and grateful for the help.' I worry about my daughters growing up in a world full of privilege with so little hardship. Will they understand the value of money and work, or will they grow up feeling entitled? It's really important to me to raise children who value respect and knowledge as opposed to money and power."

—**Laura**, mother of Alicia (seven) and Grace (four)

parenting, in the New Guinean tribes that he lived and worked with. "Allo" is a prefix derived from the Greek work *allos*, which means other or different; "allo-parents" are all the adult figures who aid parents in their job by serving as alternative parent figures to children. Diamond describes being struck by the emotional security, self-confidence, curiosity, and autonomy of members of small-scale societies—not only the adults, but also the children. He goes on to say that adolescents in these societies don't have the sorts of identity crises so common in the West because they are so tightly rooted within their families and communities.[47]

While Asian cities, with their sophisticated urban populations, are a far cry from the forests and tribes that Diamond writes about, Asian families do tend to hold on to many of these traditional practices. The "auntie–uncle" cultures of the East are still attached to the more traditional ideals of extended family networks, allo-parenting, and the care of the elderly by a family as opposed to an outside institution. As Diamond notes, when a child is jointly raised, disciplined, and loved by multiple adults, she grows up with a strong sense of belonging to a larger community. This practice not only diminishes the pressure placed on parents, but also helps children feel secure. Each child has many adult role models that he can turn to when he needs advice, support, or help. The popular saying "It takes a village to raise a child" is another way of thinking about the benefits of "allo-parenting" and traditional wisdom.

As allo-parenting is becoming increasingly endangered in the modern, developed world with its impersonal apartment buildings and fast-paced lifestyles, I think the auntie–uncle cultures of the East should try to preserve their communal orientation as much as possible. In his book *Hold On to Your Kids: Why Parents Need to Matter More Than Peers*, American psychiatrist Gordon Neufeld documents the price that families pay when they are no longer part of a cohesive community. When parents don't have a community to

47 Jared Diamond, *The World Until Yesterday: What Can We Learn from Traditional Societies?* (New York: Viking, 2012): 186–190, 208.

help them raise their kids, they become stressed and exhausted. Simultaneously, when kids don't have a strong network of supportive adults to draw on, they often turn to peers to fill the vacuum; the results can be dangerous and frightening. In his book, Neufeld examines the unraveling of families and extended communities in the US, and he paints a disturbing picture of both parents and children who find themselves floating, unanchored and adrift, like leaves tossed by the wind.

ROOTS AND SEATBELTS: Protection and restraint

No culture is perfect. Just as individualistic cultures are simultaneously liberating and isolating, auntie–uncle cultures are simultaneously comforting and restrictive–perhaps even stifling. In the last decade, many of my Indian friends who had moved to the West to study and work decided to move back to India because they wanted to be closer to their families and raise their children in their home country. Their stories about adjusting to adult life in India are always interesting and entertaining.

ASIAN PARENTS SPEAK OUT

"Small gestures of respect really count"

"I often buy my children books on Chinese stories and fables, and I make a big effort to teach them about Chinese traditions such as filial piety and Confucian values. I do think it pays off. At dinner one night, our entire extended family was sitting around a table laden with steaming-hot rice, ginger-soy steamed fish, and spicy chicken wings, which are my daughter Natalie's absolute favorite food. Even though she was only seven at the time, she didn't ask for the wings or try to help herself. Instead, she offered them to her grandparents and parents, and then waited patiently while all the elders helped themselves. Perhaps this doesn't sound like much, but I think it's those small gestures that really count. My girl is growing up to be a very considerate and respectful person, and I am so proud and happy about that."

—**Susan Chan**, mother of Cayden (twelve) and Natalie (nine)

My friend Samir left the US and moved to India to start up an office in his hometown of Chennai for his employer, a prestigious multinational company. Many of his clients are older business-men who knew his parents. In other words, Samir's clients are the "uncles" of his childhood. "It's impossible to do business with some-one when you're calling him 'uncle,'" says Samir. "You feel like a child. You automatically feel like you need to agree with everything he says. You have no power in the relationship." I asked Samir what name he uses to address these clients. "I don't call them anything. I say "Uh, um" a lot. I refuse to call them 'uncle' in a professional situation, but I also can't bring myself to use their names."

I couldn't help laughing. I've heard similar stories from other friends, too. Auntie–uncle cultures can be extraordinarily com-forting and supportive, but they also serve to solidify hierarchies in people's heads. In many ways, they probably limit intellectual growth because they prevent dissent. However, despite their limit-ing features, they are a very, very strong source of comfort and security for children and adults alike. Like a seatbelt, these net-works of relationships simultaneously comfort and stifle, protect and restrain.

In a conversation with another friend of mine who moved back to Chennai from the US, I was struck by the amount of time she spends on duties related to extended family and community. In her words, "When you move back to India, you give up your indepen-dence and freedom. All of a sudden, your mother-in-law is calling you every day to offer all kinds of advice on the children, your old aunt needs you to go out and buy her five saris by Tuesday, and your friend needs you to choreograph a Bollywood number for her wedding celebration. Everyone weighs in on every decision you make, from what you feed your children to how you should run your kitchen, and somehow everyone knows all about your life. On the one hand, it is comforting, but on the other, it can feel very restricting if you've been used to making all your own decisions in the West. You have to be a lot less selfish if you live in India. You have to constantly adjust to other people and to the community."

My Asian students echo these ideas when they talk about their families. In a discussion of East–West parenting, one of my Chinese students commented that the major difference between Eastern and Western families is that Eastern parents and aunties are "just so nosy, they always want to know what you're up to," but Western parents are "more chilled out–they let kids do whatever they want." Another student observed that in Eastern communities, words like "privacy" and "independence" just don't exist. She added that she has always been amazed by how "all the aunties somehow know everything about you." Other students described their mothers as being "very protective" of them, and supervising and monitoring them very closely.

THE PARENT-CHILD RELATIONSHIP: Filial piety and family loyalty

I have a very vivid memory of a tiny incident from my teenage years. I had just finished my freshman year of college in the US, and I was at home in Chennai for the summer. My father asked me to sign some papers. "Sign here," he said, pointing to a line, which he had marked with an X. As my eyes scanned the page, I saw lots of financial terms and numbers. I wondered what exactly I was signing, and for a brief moment, I contemplated asking my dad. Then, without asking any questions, I signed on the line.

When I thought about asking my father what I was signing, my motive was really just curiosity. I was always very, very close to my father, and I had complete and total trust in him. And I am quite sure that had I asked him questions, he would have patiently answered them without any anger or irritation. I chose not to ask any questions, however, because I had a sense deep down that questioning my father was not the right thing to do. In fact, it seemed like a hurtful thing to do. Having grown up in India, I had been imbued with the strong Indian value of filial piety. A child does not ever question her parents, because questions could be construed as a lack of trust and obedience; she is expected to put all her trust and faith in her parents and obey them completely.

"The cane was the first line of discipline"

"My husband Jerry and I show a lot of affection toward our children. We hug our children goodbye, and we give them good-night kisses. I'd say that was not commonly done one generation ago. And while we still discipline our children, we use physical punishment as a last resort. In my parents' time, the cane was the first line of discipline. I grew up being caned—and I don't hold it against my parents at all—but with our daughters, we believe that caning should be the absolute last resort. We have used it only twice in their lives. And most of my friends use the cane infrequently, more as a threat to instill fear than anything else. One of my friends has three sons…this particular friend uses the cane frequently because otherwise she finds it impossible to get the boys moving and maintain order in the home. In fact, she and her husband have big arguments about this because he thinks that the boys have grown so accustomed to the cane that they don't even care about it anymore. He would like her to reserve the cane as a 'last resort means of punishment' so that the boys take it more seriously."

—**Faith Lee**, mother of Sophia (eight) and Lily (six)

In China, too, children are expected not to question their parents. Chinese kids are raised with the expectation that they will exhibit filial piety in a variety of ways. In her book *The Three Virtues of Effective Parenting*, Shirley Yuen explains that the term for "filial piety" in Chinese is *xiao shun*, two words that have distinctly different meanings. *Xiao* means "to love and care for one's parents," while *shun* means "obedience and compliance."[48] In China, children are expected to demonstrate *xiao shun* by listening to their parents, refraining from talking back or asking questions, giving their parents part of their paychecks when they start earning money, and eventually caring for them physically, emotionally, and financially when they are old or sick.

---

48 Shirley Yuen, *The Three Virtues of Effective Parenting: Lessons from Confucius on the Power of Benevolence, Wisdom, and Courage* (Boston, MA: Tuttle Publishing, 2005): 124.

When I asked my Chinese students about the hierarchies and traditions in their families, they often tell me about their parents' insistence that they greet the elders in the family appropriately. "My mother always insists that I greet all my aunts with lots of respect in an appropriate way," says teenager Wang Fang. Clarissa, who, like Wang Fang, is Chinese, described how her family always begins meals by first serving her grandfather; after he takes a spoonful, everyone else can get their food and begin eating. *Xiao shun* and respect for elders is integral to Chinese culture. In interviews with Singaporean-Chinese mothers, I found that *every single mother,* without exception, mentioned how much they value "respect." They all insist that children greet their elders respectfully, according to Chinese tradition. One mother said that she uses the term "filial piety" and even discusses Confucian values with her children.

In both India and China, the idea of retirement homes is still viewed with skepticism and disapproval. Children are supposed to take care of their aging parents, and failing to do so is seen as immoral. When children are dutiful, they are praised and validated by the larger community, and when they fail in their filial duties, they are criticized. When my father was ill, my sisters and I took extended leave from work to spend time with him in Chennai; as a result, we earned praise and validation from the aunties and uncles we grew up with. The expectation that children must make whatever sacrifices are necessary to take care of their parents is explicitly and implicitly communicated to young people in all parts of Asia.

One of the things that surprised me about Singapore when I first moved here was the way the government tries to inculcate values in its population. Like a father determined to instill character in his children, the Singapore government has run media campaigns on everything from "racial harmony" to "kindness" to "speaking good English." In 2010, the government ran a "filial piety campaign" to remind young Singaporeans of their filial commitments. In one of the most popular filial piety ads, a young boy watches his parents care for his old, cranky, sick grandmother, and he watches his father grieve when she dies. Like a whiny child, the grandmother throws tantrums and makes life miserable for the boy's parents. Yet, despite her rude comments and constant complaints, the boy's parents are loving and dutiful in the way they care for her. The tagline is, "How one generation loves, the next generation learns." (You can watch these ads, which offer a fascinating glimpse into Asian value systems, on YouTube.) To me, this seemed to reinforce the implicit message embedded in the Bollywood movies I watched as a teenager and the Indian myths and stories I read as a child.

Similarly, the moving Chinese New Year ads run by companies as diverse as Pepsi and Bernas (a Malaysian rice company) idealize the value of filial piety. They all involve the same storyline: a grown child, firmly ensconced in the modern, globalized, work-oriented twenty-first century, is reminded of all the sacrifices that his parents made for him as a child, and is thus compelled to go home for Chinese New Year and fulfill his filial commitments.

When I spoke with Indian and Chinese parents about their expectations of their children, most of the mothers said, "If we take care of our parents well and do our duty, then hopefully our children will learn that this is the right thing to do." While I fully understand how central the ideas of filial piety and family loyalty are to Asian societies, I also wonder whether these parents are right in assuming that their children will, in fact, do for them what they have done for the older generation. As families are forced to adapt to the modern technological world characterized by two working parents, round-the-clock work hours, and tremendous geographical mobility, notions of family loyalty and filial piety, handed down from one generation to the next over millennia, may erode as quickly as they have in the West, where rapid economic development has brought with it the breakdown of the family, as seen in escalating divorce rates and the rise of single-parent homes.

While Asia's divorce rates are still significantly lower than those in the West, they are rising sharply, particularly in East Asian nations. Many economically successful Asian nations like

"I teach my girls to respect their elders"

"My parents live nearby and they come over every afternoon around 4 p.m. When they arrive, I expect my daughters to stop whatever they are doing to greet their 'Gong-Gong' and 'Ma-Ma' appropriately. These greetings are important. They teach the girls to respect their elders and value their family. Every evening when the girls return from playing outdoors, the whole family, including the grandparents, sits at the table together for dinner, and we expect good manners and respectful behavior from the children. I'd definitely call myself a 'modern Singaporean,' but I still think it's important that my daughters understand core values such as respecting elders, valuing family, and valuing Chinese culture."

—**Faith Lee**, mother of Sophia (eight) and Lily (six)

Japan and Singapore are already struggling with lower fertility rates, and fewer young people are choosing to get married.[49] Old-age homes are still rare in the East, but an increasing number of older couples are living on their own because their children have moved out of the home or moved to another city or country. (The one statistic that has remained very low in Asia is that of children born out of wedlock; according to the August 2012 issue of *The Economist,* currently less that two percent of Asian children are born out of wedlock; the numbers are far higher in the West. In Sweden, for example, 55 percent of children born in 2008 had unmarried mothers. Statistics indicate that Asians still believe that marriage and the nuclear family are integral to having children.) Looking at these figures, one has to wonder whether Asians, too, will follow in the West's footsteps as they become increasingly urbanized, modernized, and prosperous. In our modern age, can traditional social institutions such as the family coexist with modern lifestyles? Will filial piety, that age-old value so central to life in the East, slowly become an obsolete ideal?

---

49 "The Flight from Marriage," *The Economist*, August 20, 2011.

THE STORIES WE TELL AND THE SCRIPTS THEY GIVE US: Asian myths

I've always been fascinated by the value systems that dominate Asian family life, and I've spent a lot of time contemplating where those values come from. Over time, I've become increasingly convinced that much of a child's worldview is shaped in his first four or five years by the stories and sayings that he hears around him.

India and China are both lands of ancient stories that date back thousands of years. The *Ramayana* and the *Mahabharatha*, ancient Indian epics that date back to the fourth century BC, are still alive and well in India today. Unlike Greek mythology, the ancient Indian stories and religious beliefs were not replaced by the Judeo-Christian tradition or by any newer religion. Today, ancient Greek myths and epics such as Homer's *Iliad* are read and studied primarily as imaginative children's stories or academic texts. I've never encountered anyone who actually prays to Zeus or worships Poseidon. In contrast, in contemporary India, the ancient Hindu epics are very real and alive in the minds and hearts of Indians. When grandmothers tell their grandchildren about Rama and Hanuman, they truly believe in Rama's divinity and Hanuman's powers. All Indian children—and this is not an exaggeration—know the story of the *Ramayana* on some level. Kids hear these stories from their parents and grandparents, they read about them in *Amar Chitra Katha* comics, and they watch episodes of them on television. This epic is featured prominently in all Indian art forms. As a child, I remember sitting at the edge of my seat, my heart beating with anticipation, as I watched the evil Ravana trick Sita in a beautiful dance-drama at Kalakshetra, the famed Bharat Natyam dance school in Chennai. Across Indian villages, folk performances and puppet shows feature stories from the *Ramayana*. Rama, Lakshman, Sita, and Hanuman are as well known in India as Santa Claus and Spiderman are in the US.

Given the pervasiveness of the Indian epics in contemporary India, I think it would be fair to say that these stories encapsulate some of the central values that many Indians hold dear. One of the central values communicated by these myths is that of filial piety and family loyalty. In the *Ramayana*, the hero, Rama, is all set to be crowned *yuvraj* (heir to the throne) when his stepmother decides that she would rather that *her* son, Bharatha, ascend the throne. As a result, the stepmother reminds the king (Rama's father) of two wishes that he owed her because she had saved his life a long time ago when he was dying on the battlefield. She decides to redeem those two wishes, and she wishes not only that her son, Bharatha, should be the next king, but also that Rama be exiled to the forest for fourteen long years. The king falls into a faint, paralyzed: he can neither break his promise to his wife nor exile his beloved son. When Rama finds out about the situation, he absorbs the shock within himself and then calmly turns to his stepmother, touches her feet, and tells her that he will do as she says without question.[50]

Across India, Rama is revered for his unquestioning obedience to his stepmother. He ensures that his father does not have to break his promise, and he begs his brothers not to judge or condemn his stepmother for her actions. He is held up as an ideal for children across India. Rama's stepbrothers are the ideal brothers. They are absolutely loyal to Rama. The entire epic hinges on the idea of family loyalty and filial piety. These values supersede any objective sense of justice—Rama's stepmother was cruel and unjust when she exiled Rama to the forest for no fault of his own. All the same, Rama is revered for respecting her wishes. Quite simply, the epic suggests that nothing is as important as filial piety and family loyalty.

Children in India hear these stories and absorb the values, and then find that these values are reinforced everywhere: on television, at the movies, in art, in conversations. Much like the great Indian

---

50 R. K. Narayan, *The Ramayana: A Shortened Modern Prose Version of the Indian Epic*, (London: Penguin Classics, 1972): "Rama took in the shock, absorbed it within himself, and said, 'I will carry out his wishes without question. Mother, be assured that I will not shirk. I have no interest in kingship, and no attachments to such offices, and no aversion to a forest existence...My only regret is that I have not been told this by my father himself. I would have felt honored if he had commanded me directly.'"

epics, Bollywood thrives on emotional and melodramatic scenes involving parents and children. In one blockbuster movie, *Kabhi Khushi Kabhie Gham* (Sometimes Happy, Sometimes Sad), the tagline was "It's all about loving your parents," and the hero (Shah Rukh again!) is a son who becomes estranged from his parents after he marries a girl his father disapproves of. The movie ends with a tearful reunion between father and son.

It's interesting to me that filial piety is glorified so much more in the Indian epics than it is in the ancient Greek epics. In the *Odyssey* and the *Iliad*, although there are some moving father-son scenes, the heroes are not revered for being faithful to their parents. Rather, they are revered for being individualistic and fearless explorers (Odysseus) or warriors (Achilles). Fraternal loyalty is extremely important in the Greek myths; the relationships between Hector and Paris and between Menelaus and Agamemnon demonstrate the importance of brotherhood. However, none of the relationships in the *Iliad* elevate brotherhood and the obedience of a younger brother to an older brother in the way that the Indian epics do.

Chinese children, too, grow up with ancient stories that offer them particular scripts for their lives. Stories such as *The Romance of the Three Kingdoms*, *Journey to the West*, *The White Snake*, and *The Girl in the Moon* are part of the lives of most Chinese children. Andrea Li, a teacher who grew up in Qing Dao, China, says, "I heard these stories from my parents and then read them in comics—even Japanese comics have stories about Monkey, the central character in *Journey to the West*. Then I saw them on TV, in commercials and in TV series. I also read books about them. These stories really are everywhere in China."

Like the Indian epics, ancient Chinese stories also idealize the parent-child bond and glorify the value of filial piety. The *Analects* of Confucius, which date back to 400 or 500 BC, describe the importance of *xiao shun* in tremendous detail, asserting that filial piety is a basic moral tenet. Confucius urges children to move beyond mere physical or financial support for their parents and to give real reverence or *ching* (also *jing*). Furthermore, Confucius acknowledges a strong link between filial piety and order, both in the home and in the state:

> Master You [You Ruo] said, "Among those who are filial to-
> ward their parents and fraternal toward their brothers, those
> who are inclined to offend against their superiors are few
> indeed. Among those who are disinclined to offend against
> their superiors, there have never been any who are yet inclined
> to create disorder. The noble person concerns himself with the
> root; when the root is established, the Way is born. Being filial
> and fraternal—is this not the root of humaneness?"[51]

The value systems of a particular society are deeply embedded in all the stories and sayings that children hear when they are young, and they shape a person's worldview more than he realizes. I call these stories "foundational stories" because they provide people with the foundations for their worldviews and the scripts for their lives. Asian foundational stories emphasize filial piety and family loyalty, while in Western foundational stories (Homer's and Virgil's epics, Greek and Roman myths, Biblical stories from the book of Genesis, fairy tales), the emphasis lies more on individual good-ness and courage. These storylines provide a very different script for people's lives in East and West.

SECURE FAMILIES VERSUS INTELLECTUAL FREE-DOM: The Western way

There are trade-offs for everything. While the Eastern emphasis on filial piety and family loyalty tends to strengthen family ties, it prevents the questioning and exploration that are so central to Western intellectual life. In contrast, since Westerners are encour-aged to question everything (including their relationships with their

---

51 William Theodore and Irene Bloom, *Sources of Chinese Tradition: From Earliest Times to 1600* (New York: Columbia University Press, 1999).

parents, their need to obey or care for their parents, their marriages, etc.), their families are far less secure. The process of questioning can cause people to abandon the notion of family, which, much like religion, requires a certain amount of faith. Freedom from all man-made institutions, including religion and family, can lead to great intellectual leaps, but it can also leave one feeling anchorless and alone. Like blasting off into outer space or diving deep into the ocean, the thrill of exploring the unknown and living with few or no restrictions is also terribly frightening and risky.

Over the last fifty years, Western societies have begun to out-source everything that a family traditionally does: children are cared for by professionals in daycare centers, the elderly are cared for by professionals in retirement centers and nursing homes, and adults who need emotional support and comfort visit professional psychologists and psychiatrists for help. In my grandmother's generation, even in the West, all these functions were seen as the domain of the family, and specifically of women. In each family, the women were supposed to care for the children, nurse the elderly, and provide emotional comfort and support to all family members by listening to their problems and offering free counsel. Today, the Western family is far less important from a functional perspective because so many of its central roles are being performed by outside agencies. Despite the Asian commitment to traditional family structures, statistics on marriage, divorce, childcare and elder care indicate that Asian countries will probably soon follow suit.[52] In Singapore, daycare centers are becoming increasingly popular, as are counseling services. In India, one of my closest friends is in the process of starting a high-end assisted living facility for the elderly because she sees it as an increasingly pressing need. Across Asia, divorce rates have risen sharply over the last two decades.

---

52 "The Flight from Marriage," *The Economist*.
  Theresa Devasahayan and Brenda S.A. Yeoh, eds., *Working and Mothering in Asia* (Singapore: NUS Press, 2007).

TWENTY-FIRST-CENTURY ASIAN FAMILIES: Where are we headed?

What will happen to urban Asian families in the future? Will they, like their Western counterparts, become a casualty of modernization and urbanization? Authors like Jared Diamond and psychiatrist Gordon Neufeld paint a bleak picture of the consequences of abandoning family and community structures, particularly for the elderly and the young. Additionally, there is plenty of interesting research suggesting that strong family ties are extremely positive for children and adults alike. One example comes from Bruce Feiler, author of the book *The Secrets of Happy Families*, who asserts that children who grow up with a strong sense of their own family history are happier and more successful in life.

Feiler describes a study done by Dr. Marshall Duke and Dr. Robyn Fivush in 2001. The researchers asked four dozen children a series of questions about their own families. When they compared the responses to the results of psychological tests the children had taken, they reached a very strong conclusion. Children who had more knowledge of their family's history had a greater sense of control over their lives and higher self-esteem. They also had more faith in their own families, believing that their families functioned more successfully than other families. Feiler concludes that a child's knowledge of her own family's history is a very strong predictor of her psychological and emotional health and happiness. This, he says, is because family narratives give children a sense of belonging to a larger entity. They are part of a team, and their team has a long history. This sense of belonging gives a child the security she needs to make her way in a difficult world, and helps build resilience. The best narratives, according to Feiler, are those that teach a child that a family has ups and downs, but sticks together through it all.[53]

---

53 Bruce Feiler, *The Secrets of Happy Families: Improve Your Mornings, Tell Your Family History, Fight Smarter, Go Out and Play, and Much More* (New York: William Morrow, 2014).

QUESTIONS FOR TWENTY-FIRST-CENTURY GLOBAL PARENTS

How can fragmented, urbanized, Westernized families (both in Asia and the West) provide the solid, secure foundation and sense of belonging that Feiler identifies as being crucial to children's self-esteem and sense of security?

With my own children, I constantly swing back and forth between Asian scripts and Western ones, trying as always to find that balance. One potential solution to navigating the pulls of both East and West is a compromise in the middle: I tell my children that they can always ask me why I made a certain decision, and I will offer them my explanation and reasoning. However, once I have given them my explanation, they are not allowed to continue to argue or debate the situation. As their parent, as the elder who knows best and has their best interests at heart, my word is final, and no further disagreements will be tolerated. Sometimes I tighten my children's metaphorical seatbelts, requiring them to spend more time with the family and behave respectfully toward all their elders; at other times I loosen them, encouraging them to take more risks, to be more independent, and to voice their opinions and ask more questions.

The following sections suggest some practical ways of creating a supportive community for your child in the absence of a traditional extended family, and provide a list of foundational stories that will help your child appreciate both family values and the value of individual courage.

HOW TO CREATE A SUPPORTIVE COMMUNITY FOR YOUR CHILDREN

- **Socialize as a family with other families**: multigenerational socializing is healthy for kids and adults alike. Your kids should know your friends. They should have lots of "aunties" and "uncles" that they feel close to. This is important even when (actually, particularly when) they are teenagers; teens need wise and mature help, guidance, and support as they navigate high school and beyond.

- **Make sure you know your kids' friends**, and (ideally) their parents as well. This is fairly easy when children are young, but it gets harder as they get older. Neufeld argues that it is particularly important with teens, because they are most vulnerable to dangerous peer pressure—to drink, do drugs, smoke, etc.—and one way of mitigating that pressure is to know their friends and ensure that they are part of a peer community you feel comfortable with.

- **Spend a lot of time with your children** and make sure that you and the other adults in their lives (grandparents, aunts etc.) are their go-to people for questions and crises. **Their peers should never replace the older generation.** This is particularly important for adolescents, who could get very skewed advice from friends.

- **Encourage your children to greet their elders** when they walk into a room. Every Chinese mother and student I interviewed mentioned the importance of "appropriate greetings" in their culture. For example, when a parent comes home from work, children should stop whatever they are doing to greet the parent. A respectful hello and/or an affectionate hug are sufficient acknowledgement of the parent's presence and role in the child's life. Similarly, teach your children to stop whatever they are doing to stand up and respectfully greet their grandparents, aunts, uncles, and any other elder who visits. These ritualized greetings teach children to respect their elders and value their presence.

- **Make time for family meals and family outings**. Meals are especially important. Switch off the TV and make sure all family members gather around the table together for at least one meal a day to talk to each other and enjoy each other's company. Plenty of research shows that children who eat meals with their family tend to be better adjusted, happier, and more successful at school.

- **Tell your children lots of stories about their family history**. Make sure that they know about the good times and the bad times, the successes and the failures that the family has experienced. Give them a strong sense of belonging to an entity larger than just themselves. Research presented by Bruce Feiler in *The Secrets of Happy Families* shows that a strong knowledge of family history is linked to better psychological and intellectual outcomes.

- **If the grandparents live far away, encourage them to visit** for extended periods of time so that your child can develop strong relationships with them. Many of the Indian mothers I spoke with described the enormous benefits that accrue from having grandparents live in the house for extended periods of time—they can provide strong emotional support for both children and parents, and they offer a calm, wise perspective that is often lacking in the frenzied world of twenty-first-century parenting. While parents are forced to be tough disciplinarians, the grandparents can be more doting and indulgent, offering children the balance they need. Encourage the grandparents to tell your children lots of stories about the family history as well. Grandparents love doing this!

- **Make photo albums of the family** and spend time looking at the pictures together. Create a family wall with photos to remind children of the larger family that they are a part of.

- **Read and tell stories that celebrate family relationships**: Indian and Chinese myths and movies are particularly good for this purpose. Bollywood movies often idealize and glorify the parent-child relationship as well as the extended family. Chinese myths and movies present a similar view of the family, and the idea of "three generations under one roof" is revered across Asia. Much of Western children's literature also idealizes the family, from picture books like *Guess How Much I Love You* by Sam McBratney to YA books like *Wonder* by R. J. Palacio.

- **Create family rituals and traditions**, and make sure that you celebrate family events and festivals both with your extended family and with your community. Festivals like Raakhi, Diwali, the Mid-Autumn Festival, Chinese New Year, Eidh/Hari Raya, Thanksgiving, and Christmas are particularly important because they reinforce familial relationships and the importance of family.

▣ **Maintain good relationships with babysitters, nannies, daycare providers, teachers, tutors, coaches**, and all the other adults who care for your children and teach them on a daily basis. These adults—along with family and friends—will help your child know they are being cared for and guided in healthy ways. They are a crucial part of the "village" that you create for your child and for yourself, and you should work with them to help your child thrive.

A Note on Foundational Stories for Children

Authors and storytellers in every culture draw on the common literary heritage of that culture when they write or tell a story. Writers assume a certain knowledge base of foundational stories. Increasingly, as parents become more secular and global, and therefore less invested in their cultural and literary heritages, I find that students don't actually know these stories. I find myself filling in the gaps, telling them stories that I think they should have heard or read when they were young.

As a parent, if you want to give your child a strong understanding of a culture's worldview and values, and if you want to ensure that he is prepared to really understand literature from a particular culture, you should tell him these foundational stories, which have inspired and influenced children from East and West through the ages. They are one way of making your child feel more deeply rooted in his own cultural community, while also helping him to understand the universal values of goodness, courage, filial piety, and loyalty to family.

FOUNDATIONAL STORIES FROM EAST AND WEST

Foundational Stories from India

Namita Gokhale, *The Puffin Mahabharatha* (for children ages 8 to 12), Viking India, 2009

R. K. Narayan, *The Ramayana: A Shortened Modern Prose Version of the Indian Epic* (for children ages 12 and up), Penguin Classics, 1972; reprinted in 2006

Ramesh Menon, *The Ramayana: A Modern Retelling of the Epic* (for readers 16 and up), Northpoint Press, 2004

Ramesh Menon, *The Mahabharatha: A Modern Rendering* (two volumes; for readers 16 and up), iUniverse, 2006 (Note: Menon's renditions of the epics are fantastic. A wonderful read.)

Jamila Gavin and Amanda Hall, *Tales from India*, Templar Publishers, 2011

Bhakti Mathur, *Amma, Tell Me about Diwali!* Anjana Publishers, 2011 (Note: Bhakti Mathur has a whole series of lovely picture books that educate young kids about Indian festivals and Indian myths.)

Anita Ganeri, *Sikh Stories*, Tulip Books, 2014 (Note: Ganeri has written many wonderful books for young children; other titles include *Krishna Steals the Butter and Other Stories*; *Tipitaka and Buddhism*; *Islamic Stories*; and *Out of the Ark*, a collection of myths from around the world.)

Foundational Stories from China

Comic versions of *Romance of the Three Kingdoms*, AsiaPac comics

David Seow, *Monkey: The Classic Chinese Adventure Story*, Tuttle Publishing, 2005

Demi, *Buddha Stories*, Henry Holt, 1997

Rena Krasno and Yeng Fong Chiang, *Cloud Weavers: Ancient Chinese Legends* (for ages 9 and up), Pacific View Press, 2002

Ed Young, *Cat and Rat: The Legend of the Chinese Zodiac* (for preschoolers), Square Fish, 1998

Grace Lin, *Where The Mountain Meets the Moon*, Little, Brown Books for Young Readers, 2011

Foundational Stories from Europe

Ingri d'Aulaire and Edgar Parin d'Aulaire, *D'Aulaires' Book of Greek Myths* (for children ages 7 to 12), Delacorte Books for Young Readers, 1992 (reprint)

Heather Amery, *Greek Myths for Young Children*, Usborne Books, 2000

The *Graphic Myths and Legends* series published by Graphic Universe; includes titles such as *The Trojan Horse: The Fall of Troy* and *The Odyssey*

Geoffrey Horn, Arthur Cavanaugh, and Arvis Stewart, *Bible Stories for Children*, Simon & Schuster Children's Publishing, 1980 (includes stories from the Old and New Testaments)

Nursery rhyme collections

Fairytales—Cinderella, Little Red Riding Hood, Jack and the Beanstalk, Hansel and Gretel, etc.

CHAPTER 7

Twenty-First-Century Challenges for East and West: The Metaphors We Make, the Technology We Use, and the Purpose of Education

SHARED CHALLENGES IN A GLOBALIZED WORLD

Nishant, an eleventh grader, walks into school every morning bleary-eyed and exhausted. His back hunched over his laptop, eyes glued to a screen, he seems to exist in a parallel universe far from the reality of the classroom. His grades have fallen dramatically over the last year, and he's now in danger of failing the year and not receiving his high-school diploma. When I chat with him about the situation, he tells me that he finds it increasingly difficult to focus on his work. His mind is so distracted, and the screens around him so alluring. He spends hours playing video games and chatting on-line with strangers in different parts of the world; after his parents go to sleep and his house is quiet, he stays up with his laptop. When I suggest an earlier bedtime or a "screen-free day" to see whether that might help him feel a little better, he looks at me like I'm abso-lutely crazy. "I don't think I could go an hour without screens," he says, adding, "Besides, all my schoolwork is on a laptop. It wouldn't be feasible." His parents are, understandably, worried and frustrated as they watch their bright son descend into a world that they cannot rescue him from. They've tried everything they could—harsh punishments and admonitions, restricting and controlling his screen time as much as possible given that all his schoolwork requires a laptop and internet access—but nothing seems to have worked. The addiction, it seems, is too far gone.

While Nishant's addiction to his laptop is one of the more extreme cases I have encountered as an educator, many parents I meet complain about their kids' existence in parallel worlds. This particular issue seems to cut across all cultural or geographical boundaries. Kids everywhere, from San Francisco to Singapore to Seoul, spend a lot of time in front of screens, and all of us twenty-first-century parents, no matter where we live, worry about the repercussions. In East Asia, even governments are worried; the Taiwanese and South Korean governments, for example, have begun to institute laws that curtail the amount of time students spend on video games.

In conversations with parents about technology, I hear familiar complaints over and over again. One mother mused, "My teenage son says that he can do his homework, listen to music, check Facebook and write an email all at the same time. I would be so distracted, but perhaps his brain has adapted to a digital world full of multi-tasking. I wonder about the quality of work and thinking in this world. I also wonder how our children's brains are changing because of all the digital devices they use." Jenna, a Chinese mother, bemoaned the way her teenaged son and his friends spend all their time on video games. Teary-eyed, she told me that it was causing lots of friction at home. "When I told him to stop playing the other day, he turned around and yelled at me. His friends use filthy language, too. They all seem like such nice boys, but then I hear the things they're saying and doing when they're in my son's room with the door closed, and I feel so anxious. Raising teenage boys these days is so difficult. I'm very strict with my son, but sometimes I feel I'm fighting a losing battle."

It's clear to parents that technology has many benefits and is a very important part of their kids' lives, though they are rightfully nervous and worried about raising kids in a digital world. They tell me stories about all the wonders of raising kids today—a Japanese student in Singapore has weekly Skype classes with a Japanese tutor in Tokyo, kids create amazingly cool movies and presentations for their classes, the simulations that they use in their science courses help bring the subject to life, and even elementary-school kids are learning to write code and build robots. As parents and educators repeatedly remind me, the digital world is the future, and there is no skill more important for our kids than a deep understanding of and comfort with technology. Still, parents are worried. Endless negotiations about iPad time and gaming exhaust mothers. Sometimes it's much easier to give up and just let the kids play on those screens.

As an educator at a high-tech school in a high-tech city, I often have parents asking me what they should do. To be honest, I don't have the answers, and I find myself anxious about how to deal with technology in my own home. Last year, I took my son to his friend's ninth birthday party. The mom, who is a good friend of mine, invited me to stay at the party and chat with her while the boys played. As we were chatting, I noticed one boy, Jayden, playing games on his phone. He ignored the others, eyes glued to his mini-screen. When it was time to sing Happy Birthday, the birthday boy's mom said, "Jayden, put the phone away and come sing Happy Birthday." Jayden ignored her requests, as his fingers moved dexterously over the screen. It was like he was in a game-induced trance; he was so immersed in the game that he couldn't even put down the phone to sing Happy Birthday to his friend. My friend shook her head in disbelief, muttering, "Kids these days are so rude." Watching young Jayden helped reinforce my feelings about the deep need to regulate technology at home. While kids should be encouraged to engage with interesting and useful technology—like coding, robotics, and presentations or movies for school projects—their entertainment time on tablets, smartphones, video games, and laptops should be limited. If parents put these boundaries in place early on and adhere to them, kids will be a little less likely to become unhealthily addicted to screens as they grow older. And if parents are able to maintain close relationships with their kids and set strict boundaries in the early years, perhaps the teenage years will be easier.

Importantly, kids need viable alternatives to technology. They need books. (I still love old-fashioned paper books, and I think that the medium *does* matter. As Nicholas Carr argues in *The Shallows: What the Internet is Doing to Our Brains*, reading in pixels is not the same as reading in print.)[54] They need time outdoors, in nature, in the "real" world, where they can use all their senses. And they need lots of face-to-face human conversations and interactions with family and friends. Given how addictive technology can be, we, as parents, need to make the rules and do what's best for our kids. While no one really knows how best to regulate technology consumption amongst kids and teens, I think that communication and boundaries in the early years are the key to ensuring that a child grows up with a healthy relationship with technology. When I asked mothers of children under age twelve what they do to curtail screen time and regulate technology use, their answers included the following suggestions:

- No screen time on weekdays except if it's needed for homework, and regulated screen time on weekends (two hours per day on Saturday and Sunday).
- Kids need to earn screen time. If they finish all their homework and behave well, they get half an hour of screen time in the evenings.
- No screen time right before bed, as it winds kids up and is bad for the eyes.
- Get involved in the kinds of games and apps that your children use. Some of these can be very educational and interesting, while others are just mindless.
- Monitor what kinds of technology kids consume. Encourage "healthy" and "educational" technology, but limit "junk"

---

54 Nicholas Carr, *The Shallows: What the Internet is Doing to Our Brains* (New York: W. W. Norton and Company, 2010).

technology. Some games are great for kids because they build a wide range of cognitive skills, while others are mindless. Similarly, some shows are informative or thought provoking, while others are violent and dangerous for children to watch.

- Remind kids of the parallels between food and technology. Just as we teach them to eat healthy foods and minimize their consumption of junk food, we also need to teach them to consume healthy technology and minimize their consumption of junk.
- Don't let kids keep televisions and computers in their own rooms; keep the screens in more public spaces in the house so that you can maintain control over their use.
- Be strict about screen time rules; engaging in negotiations and discussions is a slippery slope. Make rules and stick to them.
- Give your child a book to read instead of an iPad when you go out and want them to be quiet.
- Don't let kids watch television or play on gadgets during meals. Engage them in conversations instead.
- Teach kids to code and get them excited about creating technology instead of just using it. Programming software packages such as Scratch, Tynker, and Mindstorms are great for young kids.
- When kids are done with their homework, send them outside to play instead of giving them the iPad.

While regulating consumption of technology is a particularly interesting challenge shared by all twenty-first-century parents, equally difficult—perhaps less talked about but no less insidious—are the messages that parents and educators continuously hear about competition and achievement. Whether you live in New York or New Delhi, you're going to be confronted by a rapidly shrinking globalized world, where your children compete not just with the kids in their school but with kids around the globe. And whether you live in Seattle or Shanghai, you're going to encounter many of the same metaphors and messages about childhood and life—metaphors created by global sports culture, corporate culture, the global education industry, and technology.

LEAVING THE GARDEN OF EDEN: Metaphors for childhood

Childhood is often romanticized in Western literature. It is a time of unlimited freedom and beauty; a utopian, Edenic paradise. Much like Adam and Eve in the Garden of Eden, children play happily in the garden of childhood, blissfully unaware of all the problems and evils that lurk in the adult world. Barefoot and splashing through puddles, children live in the moment and experience the world entirely through their senses. With ice cream smeared all over their faces and chocolate stains on their shirts, they are unconcerned about how they look or behave. In their innocence and joy, they assume that they are beautiful and lovable. As they look into our eyes for protection and assurance, they assume, too, that all adults are good people who will care for them and not hurt them.

Unfortunately, like Adam and Eve, all children will at some point eat of the forbidden fruit, gain knowledge of the adult world, and then be forced to leave their blissful paradise. As children grow up, they will inevitably encounter rejection and failure, hurt and betrayal. They will gain knowledge of troubling concepts like poverty, injustice, discrimination, and cruelty. As they experience the full range of adult emotions and experiences—love, sex, jealousy, rage, regret, hurt, betrayal, empathy, compassion, loss, grief—they will gain knowledge of good and evil, and they will, slowly but surely, be forced out of their magical garden, never to return to it again.

In Asia, too, childhood has historically been idealized and romanticized. The Confucian image of childhood as a time of purity is captured in the saying, "Children are like white paper." Across Asia, proverbs celebrate the beauty and divinity of childhood: "There is no treasure that surpasses a child," and "Until seven, children are with the gods."[55]

In Indian mythology, childhood and its beauty are often embodied in stories about the deity Krishna as a child. He would steal

---

55 Chao and Tseng, *Parenting of Asians.*

butter, play naughty pranks on the milkmaids, and constantly get himself into trouble. Yet, no one could be angry with him—partly because he was divine and partly because he was, after all, a child. Children were seen as the embodiment of innocence and joy; one was expected to laugh and smile at a child's mischief.

A particularly poetic metaphor in Eastern stories is that of a parent rowing her child across a river or helping him cross the bridge from childhood to adulthood. The river is dark and dangerous, and the parent must accompany the child on this difficult journey from innocence to experience, from immaturity to maturity. If he were to cross the river alone, he would feel sad, lonely, and scared, so it is essential that the parent experience the journey with him.[56] In that sense, many traditional Eastern metaphors for childhood center on protection: the parent must protect the child and accompany him on the journey through childhood and into adulthood.

More contemporary metaphors for childhood, not just in Asia but in big global cities around the world, seem to lack such pathos and poetry. They focus on training grounds, boot camps, battlefields, and stock markets. Children become little soldiers, wielding their laptops, pens, and backpacks, as they march to and from school and tutoring sessions, following instructions and firing out answers to test questions. Twenty-first-century life seems like a battleground to us parents: harsh, hostile, competitive and cruel. We need to train and equip our little soldiers so that they can work for a big multinational company in the future. The rhetoric in education, in both East and West, has become so corporatized that people think nothing of articles that use "What Google Needs" or "Employees of the Future" as a basis for dictating what should be taught in schools. In fact, it is big corporations, particularly technological ones, that now drive curricula and education policy.

---

56 Chao and Tseng, *Parenting of Asians.*

READY, SET, GO: Sports metaphors

I'm always surprised at the number of sports metaphors people use to describe education and childhood. Many of the parents I work with say things like, "Well, now that Aakash is in high school, he has to understand that the game is getting serious." A former student of mine, who is now a high school senior applying to colleges, recently sent me an email saying, "Senior year is so stressful. From here on it's one big race to the finish line."

In contemporary parenting and education literature, the metaphor of a race occurs repeatedly. Obama's educational initiative, "Race to the Top," suggests that the very purpose of education is to ensure that children "race" or "compete" on a global scale and win. The goal or reward seems to be economic growth for the country. Similarly, the popular documentary *Race to Nowhere*, which argued that affluent American children are working too hard, uses the metaphor of a race, albeit one with no clear finish line or purpose. Bush's controversial "No Child Left Behind" educational initiative is also

ASIAN PARENTS SPEAK OUT

"If he doesn't get into college, what will we do?"

"My cousin's son is now in high school in India. He's preparing for his grade 12 board exams, and he's studying for the IIT (Indian Institute of Technology) entrance exams. Everything seems to be a 'make or break' situation. If he doesn't get into IIT or another top-ranked engineering college, what will he do? The whole family is so extraordinarily stressed, and the stakes feel so high. The sense is that there are very few routes to successful careers, and everyone is busily grooming their children to make it into these few prestigious institutions. Asia is doing so well economically, but there aren't enough world-class Asian universities for all our highly ambitious and well-prepared children. So what are we to do? Our hope is that our children will see how hard we work and how sincere we are about our work, and they will emulate our attitude. I hope that with a good attitude and hard work, they will do well."

—**Priyanka**, mother of Nehal (six)

suggestive of a race that every kid needs to compete and finish.

Not only is parenting a competitive race, but childhood and education are, too. These races require strategy, training, and every head start that one can possibly get to beat out the competition. The prize seems to be admission to a good college, with the hopes that this will eventually lead to a successful career, financial stability, and that terribly elusive concept: happiness. Our little runners start early, and their parents spend tremendous amounts of money and time to make sure that the race is rigged in their favor.

Tarun, an Indian father I interviewed, often uses the metaphor of a tennis match when he describes his children's childhood. "These kids are playing a high-stakes match on a court that's unpredictable. They need constant practice, constant fitness training, lots of strategy, and a mind of steel. Their opponents are fierce, so they have to stay focused and play hard."

Even when people discuss educational inequity, they often use sports metaphors. When I began my teaching career with Teach For America, an organization that places college graduates in teaching positions in underserved schools across America, I often heard the phrase, "We need to level the playing field." Education is conceived of as an unfair game where rich kids have a huge head start—they know the rules of the game, they have the best equipment, they have the best coaches, and they start training very early. In contrast, poor kids can't possibly compete because they have no idea what the rules are or how to play the game, and even if we teach them the rules, they don't have the necessary equipment, and their playing fields are uneven and unmaintained. How can they ever compete in such a rigged setup? There's nothing equal about America's school districts. Some kids, through no fault of their own, end up in tough, under-resourced schools with over-burdened and disillusioned teachers; others luck out and attend elite schools where they benefit from small classes, highly qualified and motivated teachers, and every privilege and opportunity a child could possibly have. Having spent much of my life working in elite private schools, I often think that those of us who teach at such institutions, along with highly affluent parents, are the "gate-keepers of privilege." Despite our liberal biases and our desire for a more just and equal world, we make sure that wealthier students receive every advantage and privilege that money can buy, from classroom libraries to cutting-edge technology to customized academic help, and we maintain their advantages over less affluent children, widening societal inequities.

Whether we're talking about individual children, education policy, or educational inequities, we parents and educators often use the competitive world of sports as a metaphor for what we're doing. In this world, there are winners and losers, and it's every man (or child) for himself. Sometimes the thrill and pressure of the game gives children and parents a sense of purpose, a goal to work toward, and a sense of adrenaline and exhilaration. At other times, the stress and anxiety of the competition wears us out, making us feel tired, defeated, and cynical.

CORPORATE METAPHORS AND THE PURPOSE OF EDUCATION

Other oft-used metaphors in education rhetoric or "ed-speak" today seem to suggest that education and parenting are corporate activities. We *invest* in our children's futures, much as we invest in the stock markets. We look at *results*, much as bankers and industrialists look at the results of companies. We constantly hear terms like "competitive advantage," "global competition," and "payoff," which suggest the very purpose of education today is to ensure that not only individuals and their families but also nations and their economies are able to make money. In Singapore, a nation obsessed with maintaining a competitive edge in the cutthroat global marketplace, the economic and corporate language permeates the consciousness of the nation in myriad different ways: in the newspapers, on the radio, in speeches by ministers and government officials, and in education documents. Furthermore, the global emphasis on "twenty-first-century skills" suggests that the central purpose of contemporary education is only to equip our children with the many complex skills needed to *work* in the twenty-first century. Even when educators speak about "empathy" and "social skills," they do so in the context of "getting ahead" and "being successful." To be a successful worker or manager in the twenty-first century, you need to be "empathetic" and "culturally competent." We want our children to be compassionate and empathetic because these qualities will *pay off*, literally, in the long run. Even compassion and empathy, it seems, have value only because of the monetary benefits they may eventually yield.

What is the purpose of education? As an educator and a parent, I often ask myself this question. Is it, as popular parenting literature and educational rhetoric suggest, to equip children with the skills necessary to become workers in the twenty-first century's "knowledge and innovation" economy? Is it to ensure that all the big multinational companies have a steady supply of talented and qualified workers? Is it to make people and nations rich? Are schools really training and sorting grounds for universities and corporations? Is education designed to fuel cutthroat global competition?

FINDING AN ALTERNATIVE PURPOSE: Creating new metaphors

As parents and educators, we have the option of crafting an alternative purpose for our children. We can choose to educate our children to be kind and ethical people who make the world a gentler and safer place to live. We can teach them to develop a deep love of knowledge and learning, which becomes an end in itself, regardless of monetary outcomes. We can help them stay connected to their communities and to their pasts—to history, to heritage, to culture— so that they know who they are and where they come from. We can help them understand human history, with all its triumphs and its deep, troubling flaws, so that they can learn not only from past successes but also from the mistakes that humans have made over the centuries.

ASIAN PARENTS SPEAK OUT

"We are conflicted as parents"

"My children want to do things that I never thought of doing at their age. Many of my daughter's classmates at her international school have sleepovers at their friends' houses every weekend. I don't understand how parents allow their children to sleep at other people's houses—often houses where they don't even know the other child's parents—on such a regular basis. And many of these parents don't seem to care what their young girls wear or say. These kids are growing up hyper-sexualized from the time they are eight or nine. My ten-year-old daughter insists on wearing nail polish and ultra-short shorts. As a parent, it's really hard to fight these trends. My husband goes kind of wild, demanding to know why a young girl needs to wear nail polish and such short shorts. Then my daughter turns around and snaps back at us, saying that we're backwards for not letting her do things. My husband and I were both raised to respect our parents, and we find it difficult to stomach the way our daughter speaks to us. We are conflicted as parents. In fact, it's wreaking havoc in our family and in our marriage.

I really admire my Indian and Singaporean friends who are very clear about what they will or won't let their children do. As for my husband and me, we're constantly swayed this way and that, and we find parenting very challenging. We worry that if we're too strict, our children will reject us altogether, but if we're not strict enough, our children will lose their values, their identity, and their way."

—**Nandita**, mother of Sunaina (ten) and Ajay (five)

And we can help our children open up their minds so they are able to see situations from various angles and entertain perspectives that may challenge their paradigms. We can help them combat stereotypes, prejudices, and discrimination. As philosophers all the way back to Plato suggest, we can consider the larger public good of education: to build a more humane and just society. These goals are not mercenary or competitive. They are not aimed at making any person, company, or country richer. Rather, they are aimed at making our children more emotionally connected to each other and helping them live balanced and happy lives. In the twenty-first century, more than ever before, we need to step back and consider the importance of compassion, empathy, and connectedness, not because it will pay off in terms of money, but because we humans need to feel connected and cared for to be happy.

DO OUR METAPHORS MATTER?

In previous generations, where religion and community dictated values and metaphors, parents and grandparents often romanticized and idealized childhood as a beautiful, joyful time of magic and mischief. Yet today, we parents are often so anxious and stressed from long work hours and relentless demands on our time and our psyches that we become blind to the pleasure and magic of childhood. Gone are the metaphors of mischief and innocence or magical gardens. Does it matter whether we think of childhood as a magical garden, a humorous prankster, the cultivation of plant, a challenging tennis match, a corporate training session, or a hostile and bitter military training ground?

I think it does.

In many ways, our metaphors determine and dictate our parenting decisions and attitudes. If we see childhood as a time of fleeting beauty, a magical paradise that can't last, then we will probably relax a lot as parents. We will probably let our children play outside more, and enjoy watching them skipping and laughing with joy. We may be more moved by the poetry and innocence of childhood, and we may even enjoy our children's childhoods more. We may begin to see their lives as filled with possibility.

The training-ground metaphor is the less romantic and more pragmatic metaphor, for sure. It seems like the logical metaphor to use in the modern world: childhood *is* training for adulthood, and it is our responsibility as parents and teachers to make sure that our children are ready for the road ahead. We ourselves find adulthood taxing, stressful, and exhausting, and we know that as our world "develops" and "progresses," it will only become more complex and competitive. So we have to *prepare* our children, *train* them, and *equip* them for the future. If we didn't, we'd be neglecting some of our key duties as parents and teachers. While all our training may serve our children well, do we lose something in the process? Does the training-ground metaphor not only increase our anxiety about our children's future but also intensify the speed of childhood? We expect our children to start reading earlier ("What? Five already and your boy can't read?") and to start doing math earlier ("Sanaya, can you show Auntie how you can count to 50?" says a proud mother to her daughter—who is only two.)

And so many of our kids are computer literate by the time they're two. The other day, I was taking a walk in the public gardens near my apartment and I saw a baby—barely ten months old—playing with an iPad in his stroller. He could barely hold the device with his chubby baby fingers—that's how small he was—but he definitely knew how to play with it. (And on a side note, I recently read about a new baby chair by Fisher Price that allows babies to play with an iPad even if they're too young to actually hold it. It's called an "apptivity seat.") It occurred to me that we're training these kids with a fury that seems normal to us but is actually unprecedented in human history.

HOW IS TECHNOLOGY CHANGING OUR METAPHORS?
And how is it changing education and childhood?

Over the last fifteen years, I've witnessed tremendous changes in the educational world. When I first started teaching, I shared computers with my colleagues in the English department, and if I wanted to make a PowerPoint presentation, I had to send a written request to the technology department for a computer and a projector. Over the years, I saw smart-boards make their entry into classrooms, and then I saw them become obsolete with the rise of "one-to-one classrooms," or classrooms where every child has a laptop of his own.

The school where I currently work is about as cutting edge as a school can get when it comes to technology. Every student has a laptop, and all our systems—from communication with parents to reporting to homework assignments to class syllabuses—are electronic. One night, at 10 p.m., I was commenting on a student's paper on her Google document when I realized that she was editing her paper at the same time. We ended up chatting about the paper in the document itself: I made comments about areas where she needed to improve, while she asked questions and offered clarifications. From 10 to 10:30 at night, we chatted and workshopped the paper together—virtually. It struck me that I was living in a futuristic world; when I was a teenager, I could never have fathomed this kind of online interaction with a teacher about a written assignment. While this is still uncommon in most schools across the globe, it is certainly the direction in which technology is leading education.

As I try to adapt to this rapidly changing world, I often have more questions than answers. How has technology changed the way we see childhood and learning? How has it transformed our metaphors? How has it contributed to moving our conception of childhood away from magical gardens and towards corporate training sessions?

Technology is speeding everything up, and the race just got faster. It has given every child a platform to reach far beyond the confines of the classroom—or the people they know. It has connected people around the globe but ironically disconnected people within homes, families and communities. **The classroom is now global**, and the race is global too. And the world is now *flat* as a result.

It has changed our understanding of the verb "to learn." We now talk about *consuming* and *downloading* information as opposed to understanding and learning it. These verbs suggest that information and knowledge are now material goods, ready for consumption. Unlike "learn," which implies understanding of and reflecting upon information, the verb "consume" suggests that information can be bought and eaten or used easily. And unlike a long, leisurely gourmet meal to be savored and enjoyed, information is consumed as if it's fast food. We are deluged by it, and therefore we are forced to consume it as quickly as possible.

The technological revolution has also declared that consuming and downloading (i.e., learning) information is not enough; kids now have to create stuff and upload it. Twenty-first-century educators urge our children to be *uploaders, not just downloaders.* We have educational efforts like the "maker" movement, which encourages all children to make usable products as evidence of their learning. Historically, children spent years learning from masters and experts before they could begin creating for the public domain; now, the lines between adults and children have become increasingly fuzzy. Kids, too, can make and create and upload.

Technology has flipped everything around: we now have "flipped" classrooms (watch lectures on YouTube at home and then do assignments in class), "flipped" power structures (kids are in charge, and teachers are just guides on the sides), and "flipped" learning structures (create first, learn as you go). Thanks to Salman Khan and the Khan academy, children are encouraged to learn independently from the internet. In fact, in our new hyperconnected technological world, the role of teachers itself is questionable. In his much-watched TED talk about a "hole-in-the-wall experiment," Sugata Mitra, professor of educational technology at Newcastle University in England, enthusiastically declares that "any teacher who can be replaced by a machine should be." In his provocative book about twenty-first-century education, Ian Gilbert wonders, "Why do I need a teacher when I've got Google?"

Technology has changed what it means to have friends—you can "friend" thousands of people with the click of a button. (Who needs to actually invest time and energy in hanging out and chatting?) Furthermore, it has changed what we mean by *chatting* and *connecting.* I am often reminded of this when I send text messages to friends. Since I can't show my friends my feelings with a nod of my head or a smile or laugh, I have to resort to exclamations, emoticons, and shorthand like "LOL" to somehow communicate warmth in a cold and impersonal medium.

The biggest change that technology has wrought is a blurring of the lines between childhood and adulthood. Our children have access to the adult world, with all its evils and horrors as well as its knowledge and information, every time they access the internet. And they can contribute to this world in any way they want. In fact, our children are now no longer excluded from the adult world; they are invited into it and expected to participate in it even when they are very young. Technology has erased the lines between adult and child, between teacher and student, between parent and child. In a flat, egalitarian, democratic, and competitive cyber-world, kids have as much clout as adults. Our kids now leave the Garden of Eden, their magical childhood world, as soon as they know how to access YouTube and Google. The internet *is* the forbidden fruit, and two year-olds eat of it. (As one of my students once pointed out, it is no coincidence that Steve Jobs chose an apple as his company's name and symbol.) When I listen to all the new educational rhetoric— "Who needs teachers when we have Google?" and "Adults should be guides on the side, not sages on the stage"—I get the feeling that technology is creating a post-childhood world.

EDUCATIONAL METAPHORS

The rhetoric promoted by the global education industry influences educators far more than parents, but I have a feeling that at least some of it filters down to parents and families. Over the last decade, Western education research, which has had a huge influence on the East, has repeatedly exhorted teachers to be "guides on the side" instead of "sages on the stage." In fact, the idea of the teacher as an authority figure and a source of knowledge is mocked and ridiculed by the education industry on a regular basis. For millennia, families believed that teachers had a wealth of knowledge and expertise to impart to their students, but today, teachers are told to work from the sidelines, guiding and facilitating students while they learn independently or from a machine. Even in Singapore, where adults reign supreme (they are never relegated to the sidelines, but are always front and center in the classroom and in the family), the Ministry of Education espouses Western education rhetoric with campaigns and slogans such as "Teach less, learn more" (in other words, the teachers should teach less explicitly, and kids should learn more through the process of discovery and exploration).

As a parent and a teacher, I find American education rhetoric very interesting, but I question the way it is arbitrarily applied to every aspect of contemporary education. On the one hand, I am aware that ultimately, deep learning takes place when a person *actively* engages with material and constructs his or her own understanding of that material. Through fifteen years of studying and teaching in America, I gained a deep respect for the American tradition of "constructivist education," which encourages children to engage independently with texts and ideas and to construct their own understanding and interpretations. Sometimes children do learn best when a teacher steps back, relinquishes some of the power in the room, and allows students to make independent choices about their own learning. Sometimes the best discussions are almost entirely student-run; students have to frame questions, offer responses, listen to each other, challenge each other, and construct their own interpretations. Many of my students have written their best papers or made their most powerful presentations when they have chosen their own topics, crafted their own questions, and wrestled with texts and ideas on their own terms.

I'm often inspired by Kahlil Gibran's words about teaching: "The teacher who is indeed wise does not bid you to enter the house of his wisdom but rather leads you to the threshold of your own mind." Gibran's words, much like the teachings of many Western educators like John Dewey, encapsulate a powerful view on teaching that has been actively promoted and idealized in the West, particularly in America. The idea of leading a child to the very threshold of her own mind is, I think, the cornerstone of great teaching.

On the other hand, after five years of living and working in Singapore, I also have a greater appreciation for the role that the elder plays both in the classroom and at home. Children in Asia, even in a technological, post-childhood era, are still expected to obey and respect their elders. Parents in Asia feel strongly that children have a lot to learn from their elders—parents, grandparents, teachers, tutors, aunts, uncles, and elderly family friends. These elders connect children to their families and communities, to their histories and heritages, to their pasts. They offer wisdom born of experience and comfort born of love. Elders know that discipline is important, that structure is important, that guidance is important. In Asia, parents and teachers are never relegated to being "guides on the side." On the contrary, they are guides who stand at the very center of their children's lives. Children are taught to greet their parents and grandparents respectfully, to listen to and obey their elders, to show deference for the wisdom that age brings. While America is a very youth-centered society, Asia still maintains a high degree of reverence for its elderly.

Reading American rhetoric exhorting parents and teachers to empower children by giving them more choices and greater freedom (and in the process, less explicit guidance) makes me wonder whether it makes sense to marginalize the role of the elder. When the older generation fails to actively guide youngsters and instead leaves them to their own devices, aren't they abdicating a central duty that elders in communities around the world have performed for millennia: the care, teaching, and guiding of children? And when societies let machines teach children while adults stay on the sidelines, aren't they putting too much trust in these machines and devaluing their own human wisdom and expertise?

Personally, as both an educator and a parent, I would like to draw from both Western and Asian tradition and offer my students and my own children both explicit Asian-style parental and teacher guidance as well as Western-style freedom where kids can follow their own passions, make their own choices and discover things for themselves. Certain areas—core values and character education, an appreciation for one's own and others' cultural heritage, mathematical foundations, foundational reading skills (phonics), grammar and writing instruction, study skills and discipline—require more explicit guidance and instruction from parents and teachers. In contrast, when it comes to reading and analyzing literature or history, choosing topics for assignments or projects, wrestling with

"Academics and family always come first"

"I have tried to be more open and affectionate with my children, and in that sense, my parenting style was more Western. My girls can talk to me about anything—even boys and relationships. Also, I encouraged them to attend university in England, and to follow their dreams and passions as they grew older. Even though they are girls, I never told them to get married. Instead, I told them to study hard, get good jobs, and excel professionally. On the other hand, I'm very Chinese in many ways: academics and family always came first. When my children were young, I made them do supplementary academic work every Saturday morning. As a result, all three of them were not only very strong in math but also very good readers. Also, my values about money are very Chinese. I never believed in giving my girls an allowance. I told them that everything I have is for them, and I will give them everything I can. If they need money for anything, they just have to ask me. My husband and I believed that paying for their university education was our responsibility, and we never ever expected them to have to pay for it. Even now, even though they are so successful financially, I try to save everything I can so that I can leave them something substantial. For their part, they are very filial, and they always give my husband and me some part of their earnings. But we put their money into an account for them, so that they will eventually inherit it back."

—**Belinda Wong**, mother of Iris, Angie, and Penny, now in their twenties

conflicting ideas and views, engaging with the arts or with nature, experimenting with scientific concepts, and asking questions or participating in discussions, we parents and teachers need to step back and allow our children to experiment and discover, to make sense of texts and ideas independently, and to voice their opinions freely. I believe that as parents and educators there are times when we need to be "sages on the stage"—a source of authority and wisdom for our children—and others when we need to step back and remain "guides on the side," allowing our children to discover the world independently. Either way, our goal as teachers should be to lead our children to the "thresholds of their own minds."

A CULTURE OF REVERENCE, A CULTURE OF SKEPTI-CISM, AND SHARED CHALLENGES

Over my years of working both in the West and in the East, I've come to see one major cultural difference between Eastern and Western cultures that permeates education systems and child-rearing philosophies. With their emphasis on filial piety, family loyalty, respect for elders, and veneration of education and knowledge, Eastern cultures tend to encourage children to be reverent. Children are raised to be obedient and to treat family and education as sacred. In contrast, with their emphasis on questioning existing knowledge and exploring the unknown, Western cultures tend to encourage a culture of skepticism. Children are raised to ask questions, to challenge norms, and to be skeptical of existing knowledge, institutions, and authority figures. Even Eastern and Western humor differ in this regard: Western comedy tends to be far more irreverent than its Eastern counterpart. In many ways, these opposing cultures of reverence and skepticism both originate from and shape the education systems of East and West.

Despite their obvious differences in philosophy, pedagogy, and child-rearing approaches, Eastern and Western parents share an increasingly shrinking world; schools around the world draw from the same research pool, making education rhetoric around the world sound strikingly similar, at least in theory. In fact, in many of the conversations I've had with Singaporean educators and policy makers, I've heard them speak about the startling "convergence" of education rhetoric around the world. Look at any education-related website anywhere in the world, and you'll hear all the same buzzwords associated with twenty-first-century skills and twenty-first-century learners. Parents and educators around the world now share far more than they realize: the same messages, the same challenges, and the same hopes and aspirations.

Our metaphors matter. Our values matter. As we try to raise and educate children in a globalized and technological world that seems to value money, competition, and economic progress above all else, we may want to consider the impact of technology on our kids and the metaphors we use to think about childhood. As we struggle to build strong relationships with our children and help them develop healthy relationships with the devices and machines that increasingly rule all of our lives, we need to consider the boundaries we put in place early on. Do we want to give up thinking about childhood as a magical, joyous time to be treasured and protected? Are we so anxious that we are unable to enjoy our children's childhood? As parents and educators, we can create our own metaphors and find our own balance between sharing our wisdom and experience with our children and giving them the space and time to discover and experience the world independently.

Looking Back and Looking Forward

People are made of places. They carry with them
hints of jungles or mountains, a tropic grace
or the cool eyes of sea gazers.
                    —*Elizabeth Brewster,* "Where I Come From"

A short while ago, toward the end of my fifth year of teaching in Singapore, I was chatting with a British colleague at work. She mentioned that her young son was struggling with some of his schoolwork, and I commiserated with her, telling her that my son, too, had been struggling with a particular unit in one of his classes. "How do you deal with it?" she asked me. Without really thinking about my response, I answered honestly, "I tell him that he's got to practice more and work harder." She started laughing, and said, "I tell my son that no one can be good at everything, so he should do his best but not worry about it." Then, with a smile, she added, "You're such an Asian mom." Perhaps I am, I thought. When I left America, I was very much an American mother, but after five years in Singapore, perhaps I have become an Asian mom.

It has been five years since I arrived on this tropical island of searing sun, bright bougainvillea, and beautiful beaches. I find my-self slipping effortlessly into Singlish, the local variant of English, and wondering at the way we humans adapt to places, breathing in not just the air but the culture and the language. What surprised me five years ago seems perfectly normal now; what seemed exotic then seems ordinary now.

America gave me many things that I have held onto, and perhaps I have come to appreciate them more now that I am oceans away from the US. I have held onto the conviction that reading for pleasure matters tremendously and children must grow up in a world rich with books and imagination. I have held onto my idealization of childhood play and the need for freedom and unstructured time. I have held onto my admiration for America's "Yes, we can" culture and the freedom it affords parents, children, and educators to think and act creatively.

Yet, along with my sweaters and boots and my American accent, I also gradually lost or discarded some of the notions that seemed so central to my parenting and teaching philosophy when I lived in the US. Under the Singapore sun, surrounded as I am by Asian culture, I find myself making different assumptions about parenting and teaching. I don't worry so much about children's self-esteem, and I assume kids and their parents are strong enough to engage in honest conversations about their work, their efforts, and their behavior. As a parent, I no longer lavish unnecessary praise on my children, and I don't think twice about telling them that they have to practice harder, put in more effort, do another draft of their writing, or behave more respectfully. My scripts have changed; they now frequently include words like "respect" and "practice." While I'm still not a particularly strict mother, I'm a lot stricter now than I was when I was in the US, and in many ways I feel Singapore has empowered me as a parent. I feel more sure of myself and more confident about my own authority as a parent and an educator.

I have also gained a newfound respect and interest in mathematics, and I think much more about creating a math-rich culture in my home than I ever did when I lived in the US. I enjoy doing math with my children, and I know for a fact that I would not have emphasized math this heavily as a parent had I stayed on in the US. Similarly, I spend a lot more time considering how to help my own children as well as my students extend their attention spans and deepen their focus, instead of merely accommodating limited attention spans. My views on respect, practice, attention, focus, and discipline have altered considerably; where I saw these as limitations and constraints when I was in the US, I now see them as essential both for deep learning and for a harmonious family environment.

As an educator, too, I find that my views have changed. When I arrived in Singapore five years ago, I thought that national exam systems were oppressive; now, while I still sometimes chafe at their restraints, I also see value in these systems as they not only give both students and educators a clearly defined common purpose but also ensure mastery of key skills and content areas. By holding *students* accountable, national exam systems encourage them to study hard and demand excellence of themselves. Similarly, where my years in America had convinced me that memorization was an impediment to learning, that it was wrong as an educator to demand that students memorize anything, my years in Singapore have helped me regain a reverence for the power of human memory, and I now see memorization and knowledge as prerequisites for deep understanding and critical thinking.

Some things, however, are true no matter where we raise our children, and I hope that wherever my travels take me and whatever kind of mom or educator I evolve into, I will always value these central ideas. Most parents in the East and the West—in every corner of the world—want the same long-term outcomes for their children. We all feel a deep desire to ensure that our children are healthy and happy, and we all want them to be kind and compassionate to others, to be good people who act with integrity to make the world they live in a better, more humane place. I often tell my own children and my students that while academic skills are important, nothing is as important as being kind and ethical, and the ultimate goal in life is not achieving a perfect score but finding fulfillment and happiness in our relationships and our work.

In conclusion, as parents striving to raise our children in a globalized world, we all have a lot to learn from each other. As parents we don't have to choose one school of thought or another; instead, we can seek to balance opposing ideals as well as possible. Emphasize reading *and* math, find a balance between freedom *and* structure, encourage children to speak up and ask questions, but *also* remind them to be respectful of their elders. And most importantly, as the world flattens and shrinks and we all share more than we ever did before, we need to reshape our own metaphors for what childhood and education are all about and remember to emphasize kindness and empathy, and to raise children who will be resilient and strong, ready to face the challenges that life will throw at them.

ACKNOWLEDGEMENTS AND THANKS

Firstly, I would like to thank all the parents, students, and educators who shared valuable insights with me, both formally and informally over the last five years. To all the mothers—thank you so much. Without your stories, this book wouldn't exist.

In particular, a very special thank-you to the following people for their valuable contributions, help and support.

Nayantara Srinivasan
Daphne Lee
Wendy Kang
Gillian Heng
Sara Tan
Joanne Li
Wu Guang Li
Qing Liu
Alpa Raiyani
Kamaljeet Hayer
Mathangi Venkatesh Babu
Sonali Sethi Jain
Mrs. Sengupta
Gunjali Singh
Vrishali Shekar
Sraboney Ghose
Melinda Foong
Norrida Bte Mohd Salleh
Siti Maslinda Binte Mohd Sallim
Eileen Kang
Shane Kwek (Innova Junior College)
Dr. Jason Tan (National Institute of Education, Singapore)
Dr. Gavin Jones (National University of Singapore)
Dr. Kirpal Singh (Singapore Management University)
Clarinda Choh (Head of GEP, Hwa Chong Institution)

I would also like to thank my fantastic agent, Helen Mangham, for being such a solid source of support through the entire process. Additionally, Jayapriya Vasudevan also provided encouragement and advice along the way.

To my editor, Cathy Layne, a big thank-you for your deep investment in my book and for all the constructive feedback. Also, I would like to thank the entire team at Tuttle for believing in my book.

Over the last year, I have received huge amounts of feedback from a number of friends and colleagues. Specifically, I would like to thank Nadine Bailey, Carol Lam, Kate Levy, and Chris and Shasta Huntington for taking the time to read parts of my manuscript and offer feedback. Also, thank you to Sandhya and Shaan, my close friends from Chennai, for encouragement along the way.

I would also like to thank all my students—past, present, and future—for enriching my life so much. A very special shout out to the many students who shared their stories with me. Thanks to Ashley, Ada, Fiona, Amanda, Vanessa, Minjin, and all the other kids who made this book possible.

I would like to thank my family. My father, the late Raj Thiagarajan, and my mother, Debbie Thiagarajan, have also always been a source of intellectual and creative inspiration. My sisters, Tara and Rena, have always been my closest friends. I am eternally grateful for all the love, support, and guidance that my parents and sisters have given me.

To my dear husband, Ritwik, thank you for supporting me through this process in so many ways: from offering me emotional support to reading my manuscript and offering me constructive feedback.

And most importantly, to Lekha and Rishi, my darling children, a big hug for bringing so much love and laughter into my life and a big thank-you for inspiring me to write this book.

BIBLIOGRAPHY

CHAPTER 1
WHY ARE ALL THE ASIAN KIDS ON THE MATH TEAM?

Books:

Boaler, Jo. *What's Math Got To Do With It?* New York: Viking Penguin, 2008.

Dehaene, Stanislas. *The Number Sense: How the Mind Creates Mathematics*. New York: Oxford University Press, 2011.

Eliot, Lise. *Pink Brain, Blue Brain: How Small Differences Grow into Troublesome Gaps—and What We Can Do About It*. New York: Houghton Mifflin Harcourt, 2009.

Gladwell, Malcom. *Outliers: The Story of Success*. New York: Little, Brown and Company, 2008.

Schank, Roger. *Teaching Minds*. New York: Columbia University Press, 2011.

Steele, Claude. *Whistling Vivaldi: How Stereotypes Affect Us and What We Can Do*. New York: W. W. Norton & Co., 2010.

Other sources:

Claessens, Amy, and Mimi Engel. "How Important Is Where You Start? Early Mathematics Knowledge and Later School Success." *Teachers College Record* 115 (June 2013).

Intel Science Competition website: http://www.intel.com/content/www/us/en/education/competitions/science-talent-search.html.

Levine, Susan C., Linda Whealton Suriyakham, Meredith L. Rowe, Janellen Huttenlocher, and Elizabeth A. Gunderson. *Developmental Psychology* 46, no. 5, September 2010. doi: 10.1037/a0019671.

Li, Hao. "Asian Americans Increasingly Defy STEM Stereotypes." *International Business Times*, August 6, 2010. http://www.ibtimes.com/asian-americans-increasingly-defying-stem-stereotype-246578.

Math Counts website: http://mathcounts.org/.

Ma, Ying Yi. "Model Minority, Model for Whom? An Investigation of Asian-American Students in Science and Engineering." *AAPI Nexus: Aisian Americans & Pacific Islanders Policy, Practice, and Community*, UCLA Asian American Studies Center, September 19, 2011.

Qiang, Gu Yong. "In China, Higher Education Brings Few Guarantees." *Time*, July 14, 2013.

CHAPTER 2
RAISING READERS–IS WEST REALLY BEST?

Books:

Hart, Betty, and Todd R. Risley. *Meaningful Differences in the Everyday Experience of Young American Children.* Baltimore, MD: Paul H. Brookes, 1995.

Kittle, Penny. *Book Love: Developing Depth, Stamina, and Passion in Adolescent Readers.* Portsmouth, NH: Heinemann, 2013.

Krashen, Stephen D. *The Power of Reading: Insights from the Research.* Portsmouth, NH: Heinemann, 2004.

Wolf, Maryanne. *Proust and the Squid: The Story and Science of the Reading Brain,* New York: HarperCollins, 2007.

Other sources:

The Annie E. Casey Foundation. "Early Warning Confirmed: A Research Update on Third-grade Reading." Baltimore: The Annie E. Casey Foundation, 2013. http://www.aecf.org/resources/early-warning-confirmed/.

Anderson, Richard C. and William Nagy, "The Vocabulary Conundrum," in *The Professional Journal of the American Federation of Teachers* 16, no. 4 (1992).

Cunningham, Anne. E., *and* Keith E. Stanovich. "Early Reading Acquisition and Its Relation to Reading Experience and Ability 10 Years Later. *Developmental Psychology* 33 no. 6 (November 1997): 934–945.

Kidd, David Comer, and Emanuele Castano. "Reading Literary Fiction Improves Theory of Mind." *Science* 342 (October 2013): 377–380.

Kim, James S. "Summer Reading and the Ethnic Achievement Gap." Paper presented at the American Educational Research Association, Chicago, April 21, 2003.

Kim, James S. "Research and the Reading Wars." In *When Research Matters*, edited by Fredrick M. Hess, 89–111. Cambridge, MA: Harvard University Press, 2008.

Krashen, Stephen. "We Acquire Vocabulary and Spelling by Reading: Additional Evidence for the Input Hypothesis." *Modern Language Journal* 73 (1989): 440–464.

Krashen, Stephen. "School Libraries, Public Libraries, and the NAEP Reading Scores." *School Library Media Quarterly* 23 (1995): 235–238.

McQuillan, Jeff, and Victoria Rodrigo. "Literature-Based Programs for First Language Development: Giving Native Bilinguals Access to Books." In *Literacy, Access, and Libraries among the Language Minority Population*, edited by Rebecca Constantino. Lanham, MD: Scarecrow, 1998.

Nagy, William, Richard Anderson, and Patricia Herman. "Learning Word Meanings from Context during Normal Reading." *American Educational Research Journal* 24 (1987): 237–270.

Paul, Annie Murphy. "Why Third Grade is So Important: The Matthew Effect." *Ideas* (*Time* magazine's blog), September 26, 2012. http:///ideas.time.com/2012/09/26/why-third-grade-is-so-important-the-matthew-effect/.

Ramos, Francisco, and Stephen Krashen. (1998) "The Impact of One Trip to the Public Library: Making Books Available May Be the Best Incentive for Reading. *The Reading Teacher* 51, no. 7 (April 1998): 614 - 615

Shu, Hua, Richard C. Anderson, and Houcan Zhang. "Incidental learning of word meanings while reading: A Chinese and American cross-cultural study." *Reading Research Quarterly 30, no.*1 (1995), 76–95.

Stanovich, Keith E., Richard F. West, and Michele R. Harrison. "Knowledge growth and maintenance across the lifespan: The role of print exposure." *Developmental Psychology* 31, no. 5 (September 1995): 811–826.

Stanovich, Keith E., and Anne Cunningham. "Studying the consequences of literacy within a literate society: the cognitive correlates of print exposure." *Memory and Cognition* 20, no. 1 (1992): 51–98.

Stanovich, Keith E., and Anne E. Cunningham. (1993) "Where does knowledge come from? Specific associations between print exposure and information acquisition." *Journal of Educational Psychology* 85, no. 2 (1993): 211- 229.

Sternberg, Robert. "Three Basic Facts about Vocabulary." In *The Nature of Vocabulary Acquisition*, edited by Margaret G. McKeown and Mary E. Curtis, 89. New York: Psychology Press, 2014.

CHAPTER 3

MEMORIZATION, PRACTICE, EXAMS AND OTHER THINGS THAT ASIANS LOVE

Books:
Carr, Nicholas (2011) *The Shallows: What the Internet Is Doing to Our Brains*. W. W. Norton and Co.

Dalrymple, William. *Nine Lives: In Search of the Sacred in Modern India*. New York: Vintage Books, 2011.

Dehaene, Stanislas. *Reading in the Brain: The New Science of How We Read*. New York: Penguin Books, 2009.

Foer, Joshua. *Moonwalking With Einstein: The Art and Science of Remembering Everything*. New York: Penguin Books, 2011.

Li, Jin. *The Cultural Foundations of Learning: East and West.* New York: Cambridge University Press, 2012.

Park, Hyunjoon. *Re-evaluating Education Systems in Korea and Japan: De-mystifying Stereotypes.* New York: Routledge, 2013.

Willingham, Daniel T. *Why Don't Students Like School? A Cognitive Scientist Answers Questions about How the Mind Works and What It Means for the Classroom.* San Francisco: Jossey Bass, 2009.

Wolf, Maryanne. *Proust and the Squid: The Story and Science of the Reading Brain,* New York: HarperCollins, 2007.

Other sources:

Teng, Amelia. "Interesting, Tricky PSLE Science Paper Scores Well." *The Straits Times,* October 12, 2013.

CHAPTER 4

WHERE ARE ALL THE CHILDREN?

Books:

Cather, Willa. *My Antonia.* Boston: Houghton Mifflin, 1918.

Gilbert, Ian. *Why Do I Need a Teacher Now That I Have Google?* New York: Routledge, 2010.

Golinkoff, Roberta, and Kathy Hirsch-Pasek. *Einstein Never Used Flashcards: How Our Children Really Learn—and Why They Need to Play More and Memorize Less.* Emmaus, PA: Rodale, Inc., 2004.

Kahn, Salman. *The One World Schoolhouse: Education Reimagined.* London, England: Hodder & Stoughton, 2012.

Louv, Richard. *Last Child in the Woods: Saving our Children from Nature-Deficit Disorder.* Chapel Hill, NC: Algonquin Books, 2008.

Wilson, Edward O. *Biophilia.* Boston: Harvard University Press, 1984.

Other sources:

Chao, Ruth, and Vivian Tseng. "Parenting of Asians." In *Handbook of Parenting* vol. 4 ("Social Conditions and Applied Parenting"), edited by Marc H. Bornstein. Mahwah, NJ: Lawrence Erlbaum Associates, 2002: 50–93.

Davie, Sandra. "NIE Studying Impact of Tuition," *The Straits Times,* September 28, 2013.

Park, Alice. "Why Up To 90 % of Asian Schoolchildren Are Nearsighted." *Time* Magazine, May 7, 2012. http://healthland.time.com/2012/05/07/why-up-to-90-of-asian-schoolchildren-are-nearsighted/

Scheider, Barbara, and Yongsook Lee. "A Model for Academic Success: The School and Home Environment of East Asian Students."

Anthropology & Education Quarterly 21 (1990): 358–377. doi: 10.1525/
aeq.1990.21.4.04x0596x. "Asian Spending Billions on Tutors," *AFP* article, July 5, 2012. http://sg.news.yahoo.com/asia-spending-billions-
tutors-study-223633801.html.

CHAPTER 5
RAISING RESILIENT CHILDREN: how do we deal with Failure?

Books:
Boaler, Jo. *What's Math Got To Do With It?* New York: Viking Penguin, 2008.

Dweck, Carole. *Mindset: The New Psychology of Success.* New York: Random House, 2006.

Fox, Jennifer. *Your Child's Strengths: A Guide for Parents and Teachers.* New York: Penguin Press, 2008.

Hernandez, Michele. *A is for Admissions: The Insider's Guide to Getting Into the Ivy League.* New York: Hachette Book Group

Levine, Mel. *A Mind at a Time: America's Top Learning Expert Shows How Every Child Can Succeed.* New York: Simon and Schuster, 2002.

Li, Jin. *The Cultural Foundations of Learning: East and West.* New York: Cambridge University Press, 2012.

Segal, Nancy. *Born Together, Reared Apart.* Cambridge, MA: Harvard University Press, 2012.

Other sources:
"Child Suicide amongst Singapore Kids." *The Asian Parent* magazine, September 25, 2012. "China: Student suicide concerns grow." *University World News* 78, May 31, 2009. http://www.universityworldnews.com/articlephp?story=20090528172303439.

Davie, Sandra. "Singapore Teens Rank #1 in Problem Solving." *The Straits Times*, April 2, 2014.

Loon, Ho Kong. "Parents and Teachers Need to Work Together." *The Straits Times*, May 12, 2014. http://sg.theasianparent.com/singapore_children_suicide_depression/

Toga, Arthur W. and Paul M. Thompson. "Genetics of Brain Structure and Intelligence." *Annual Review of Neuroscience* 28 (2005), 1–23.

"Worry Over High Student Suicide Rate in India." First published in *The New Paper*, Sunday, Feb 7, 2010. http://news.asiaone.com/News/Education/Story/A1Story20100205-196894.html.

CHAPTER 6

MYTH AND MEDIA: The Stories We Tell and The Scripts They Give Us

Books:

Devasahayan, Theresa, and Brenda S. E. Yeoh, editors. *Working and Mothering in Asia*. Singapore: NUS Press, 2007.

Diamond, Jared. *The World Until Yesterday: What Can We Learn from Traditional Societies?* New York: Viking Press, 2012.

Feiler, Bruce. *The Secrets of Happy Families: Improve Your Mornings, Rethink Family Dinner, Fight Better, Go Out and Play, and Much More*. New York: William Morrow, 2013.

Narayan, R. K. *The Ramayana: A Shortened Modern Prose Version of the Indian Epic*. London: Penguin Classics, 1972.

Neufield, Gordon, and Gabriel Maté. *Hold On To Your Kids: Why Parents Need to Matter More Than Peers*. New York: Ballantine Books, 2005.

Theodore, William, and Irene Bloom. *Sources of Chinese Tradition: From Earliest Times to 1600*. New York: Columbia University Press, 1999.

Yuen, Shirley. *The Three Virtues of Effective Parenting: Lessons from Confucius on the Power of Benevolence, Wisdom, and Courage*. Boston: Tuttle Publishing, 2005.

Other sources:

"The Flight from Marriage." *The Economist*, August 20, 2011.

CHAPTER 7

THE METAPHORS WE MAKE, THE TECHNOLOGY WE USE, AND THE PURPOSE OF EDUCATION

Books:

Carr, Nicholas. *The Shadows: What the Internet is Doing to Our Brains*. New York: W. W. Norton and Company, 2010.

Other sources:

Chao, Ruth, and Vivian Tseng. "Parenting of Asians." In *Handbook of Parenting* vol. 4 ("Social Conditions and Applied Parenting"), edited by Marc H. Bornstein. Mahwah, NJ: Lawrence Erlbaum Associates, 2002: 50–93.